# Expanding Horizons of Human Rights

# Expanding Horizons of Human Rights

*Edited by*

Subrata Sankar Bagchi

**ATLANTIC**

PUBLISHERS & DISTRIBUTORS (P) LTD

Published by

**ATLANTIC**

**PUBLISHERS & DISTRIBUTORS (P) LTD**

7/22, Ansari Road, Darya Ganj,
New Delhi-110002
Phones : +91-11-23273880, 23275880, 23280451
Fax : +91-11-23285873
Web : www.atlanticbooks.com
E-mail : info@atlanticbooks.com

Branch Office
5, Nallathambi Street, Wallajah Road,
Chennai-600002
Phones : +91-44-64611085, 32413319
E-mail : chennai@atlanticbooks.com



ISBN 978-81-269-1069-4



Printed in India at Nice Printing Press, A-33/3A, Site-IV,
Industrial Area, Sahibabad, Ghaziabad, U.P.

# Acknowledgements

At the very outset I would like to express my deep gratitude to each of the distinguished contributors to this volume who have been very helpful and extremely cooperative in making their valuable contributions. I am also thankful to the University Grants Commission of India for funding the seminar in which the papers were presented. I would also like to extend my thanks to the Bangabasi Evening College authorities, particularly our former principal Dr. Jyoti Prakas Haldar, Teacher-in-Charge, Sri Amalendu Chatterjee and our present Principal Dr. Ratan Kr. Bannerjee for lending helping hands to conduct the seminar as well as to publish this edited volume.

I would also like to express my heartfelt gratitude to all my colleagues for their active cooperation and generous support. Among them Dr. Nibedita Chakrabarti, Babul Kr. Paul, Dr. Pradip Kr. Dey, Prasanta Maity, Siddhartha Das Gupta, Pitam Ghosh, Sujata Chatterjee, Swarupa Chatterjee, Dipak Dey, Swapan Kr. Ghosh and Dr. Jyotsna Chatterjee have been very active and have worked hard to make the event successful. In this connection, I must specially mention the contribution of my colleague Barnana Bhowmick who helped me immensely during the editing of this volume. I would also like to thank the members of the non-teaching staff of the college, for their cooperation particularly Jahar Lal Das, Kallol Das Gupta, Asit Maity, Bhaskar Nandi and Dhupnarayan Singh. I am also thankful to my students who have worked hard to make the seminar successful.

I am extremely grateful to Atlantic Publishers and Distributors (P) Ltd. for publishing the book. I am also thankful to Dipak Shome for typing some part of the manuscript. Last but not least, I express my sincere thanks to my beloved niece Urmi for providing me with some nice moments of distraction which offered much-needed relaxation during the compilation of this collection of papers.

**Subrata Sankar Bagchi**

# Preface

Human rights have been a cynosure of study for a very long time as we find mentions of human rights in such texts as the Babylonian Code of Hammurabi, the juridical rulings of the ancient Israeli Sanhedrin banning torture and limiting the use of capital punishment, the Islamic legislation on rights of women, our own Vedic tradition of seeing the logic of the opponent before our own, the English Magna Carta, the US Declaration of Independence, the nineteenth century conventions outlawing the slave trade and the post-World War II Universal Declaration of Human Rights (UDHR). As we all know, with the enactment of UDHR, human rights issues began to take a more formal shape and the provisions laid down in UDHR became formally binding for each of those countries which were signatories to it.

Despite the provisions laid down in UDHR, the International Bill of Human Rights and various international treaties, intense political discussion has continued over the scope and content of the human rights canon to be promoted, especially within the areas of international development and globalisation. At present, political debate is focusing on the possibility of legally enforcing those obligations embodied in the International Pact for Economic, Social and Cultural Rights, including, for instance, access to food, water, education and housing, but is equally concerned with finding suitable instruments that would allow the human rights approach to be anchored in development policy. But this debate has now been taken over by the questions like *who* is prescribing *what,* the kind of rights required for *whom,* in *which* capacity and *why*? These neo-colonial debates have actually expanded the horizons of human rights and taken the concept to a new level.

This book is based on the deliberations of a two-day UGC-sponsored seminar titled "Expanding Horizons of Human Rights" (18th and 19th September 2007), organised to discuss various issues relating to new and emerging fields of human rights. The panel of speakers who delivered lectures in this seminar were mostly stalwarts in their respective fields. This book is a collection of papers from those erudite scholars who attended the seminar and made their valuable contributions to it.

I sincerely hope that the book will help in disseminating knowledge on human rights in society. I also hope that it would prove to be a useful publication for the students and teachers of human rights and researchers in this field.

**Subrata Sankar Bagchi**

# Contents

# Expanding Horizons of Human Rights

1

*Subrata Sankar Bagchi*

The scope of human rights is expanding significantly now with its effect reaching to various hitherto unexplored areas of mankind. The basic intention of this collection of papers, based on the contributions made by the speakers in a UGC-sponsored seminar held during 18th and 19th September 2007 in Bangabasi Evening College (University of Calcutta) of Kolkata, is to highlight some of the major aspects of this vast area of knowledge.

Historically speaking, issues related to rights of different section of populations kept on surfacing since the inception of civilisations in different parts of the world. There are ample evidences in the history of all the great civilisations throughout the world that many people were unsatisfied with the notion that right or good is simply what a particular society or ruling elite feels is right or good at any given time. Human rights actually emerged from the notion of 'natural rights' of the classical Greek philosophers like Aristotle and Aquinas. But this emergence did not come without opposition, as some argued that rights could only emerge from the law of a particular society and could not come from any natural or inherent source. Nevertheless, the moral authority of natural rights was assured because it had divine authorship since this political thought was almost entirely based on Christian religious tenets. Perhaps Thomas Hobbes posed the first major assault in 1651 on the divine basis of natural right by describing a State of Nature in which God did not seem to play any role. Later we find that Kant's doctrine based on his moral philosophy emphasised that a state had to be organised through the imposition of, and obedience to, laws that applied universally; nevertheless, these laws should respect the equality, freedom, and autonomy of the citizens. In his doctrine, he also prescribed some basic rights necessary for civil society. Locke, on the other hand, defended the divine basis of natural right with several references to what God had ordained or given to mankind. Locke's doctrine had a lasting influence on the American Declaration of Independence and France's Declaration of the Rights of Man and the Citizen. Thomas Paine in his two volume book in 1791 and 1792 entitled *The Rights of Man* made a distinction between *natural* rights and *civil* rights, but he continued to see a necessary connection. Paine's view was inspired by Rousseau's social contract view which argues that people agree to live in common if society protects them and their rights as individuals cannot defend them on their own.

Modern theories on human rights developed a notion of natural rights that draws inspiration from the secular natural rights trend of Paine and Rousseau. In a further extension of the natural rights tradition, human rights are now often viewed as arising essentially from the nature of humankind itself. Opposition to this view argue that rights do not exist independently of human endeavour; they can only be created by human action. In this vein, Karl Marx also left a legacy of opposition to rights as he denounced rights as a fabrication of bourgeois society, in which the individual was divorced from his or her society; rights are needed in capitalist states in order to provide protection from the state.

Thus, the history of thought on human rights has been one of several centuries of debate and acrimony. But we are yet to answer the concerns raised by the earlier thinkers—are rights truly the product of a particular vision and laws of a society? Or, are human rights so inherent in humanness that their origins and foundations are incontestable? Another important debate on the history of human rights theories is whether it can overcome its affinity with the values of Western liberalism from which it emerged. One must emphasise that in order to enjoy universal legitimacy human rights must have a basis that survives charges of ideological imperialism.

But without fully universal human rights, one is left simply trying to assert that one's own way of thinking is better than somebody else's. The prime rhetorical benefit of human rights is that they are viewed as being so basic and fundamental to human existence that they should surpass any other consideration. Thus, the effort of a universal definition of human rights emerged in the Universal Declaration of Human Rights adopted and proclaimed by the General Assembly of the United Nations, 1948. Included among these are the right to life, liberty and security; the right not to be discriminated against on the basis of race, colour, sex, language, religion, social class or political opinion; the right to vote, freedom of speech and freedom of press; the right to be free from arbitrary invasion of privacy, family or home; and legal rights such as the right to due process of law and the presumption of innocence until proven guilty. This declaration highlighted the universality and the centrality of humanity of achieving individual freedom as the ultimate goal of the new rights movement. This view of human rights owes allegiance to the premise that is based on respect for the dignity and worth of all human beings and seek to ensure freedom from fear and want. Rooted in ethical principles (and usually inscribed in a country's constitutional and legal framework), human rights are essential to the well-being of every man, woman and child. Premised on fundamental and inviolable standards, they are considered as universal and inalienable.

After the Second World War, this traditional view of human rights has been repeatedly challenged. Some say that it is too limited in scope and that a more multidimensional and holistic approach must be taken. Consequently, through various instruments, charters and declarations, the basic civil and political rights have been expanded to include crucial social, economic and cultural rights. These include: the right to an adequate standard of living; the right to education; the right to work and to equal pay for equal work; and the right of minorities to enjoy their own culture, religion and language. Of particular importance to this view is the protection and advancement of the rights of disadvantaged and minority groups (such as women, children and indigenous peoples). Along with these treaties and covenants we find various rule of law imperatives and economic linkage requirements in which every nation is being required by international lending agencies like the IMF and the World Bank to become aligned with such human rights imperatives represented as universal in structure, form and purpose.

Let us now come back to the debate on the universality and inalienability of human rights. Human rights are considered universal as they are said to belong to all humans in every society and human rights are supposed to be inalienable because they flow from and protect human existence, they cannot be taken away without endangering the value of that existence. On the one hand, if universality argument agrees human rights as having some existence independent of human creation it would be argued that such independent moral standards may lead to an indication towards a divine origin for universal human rights which might not be acceptable as a legitimate argument, since there is no one God that is recognised universally. On the other hand, some observers consider human rights as the creations of human intellect by gradual growth of consensus building around norms of behaviour that eventually acquire an obligatory character but it is difficult to trace the epistemological origins of this consensus. Human rights is also considered created through a conscious attempt to create binding rules of behaviour and with the joining of more individuals or state governments this may lead the development of international agreements on human rights. This approach also has its share of criticism as with any inception of human rights, one is faced with having to acquire acceptance of their authority and it is not guaranteed that everyone will share the same motivation or inspiration for human rights. Human rights are agreed to exist because a majority says they do. But what of the minorities who object to the concept of universal human rights, or when a minority sincerely believes that some benefit being deliberately denied them by the majority. Any body of knowledge on human rights which claims some degree of inclusion would have to go through these debates.

Theories on human rights have also disagreed on the universality and inalienability of human rights as each approach to human rights has different strengths and vulnerabilities in facing the challenges posed by relativists and utilitarianists. Most pervasively held school of thought on human rights, advocated by the Western liberals and reflected in the UN declarations on human rights, considers that human rights exist in order to protect the basic dignity of human life. But the inherent weakness of this approach lies in trying to identify the ideal nature of dignity which is very much a moral choice and there is every possibility that one particular conception (in this case the conception of the Western liberals) prevailing over other views of dignity. While the Western liberalism holds that all humans are equal and the dignity of every individual is to be considered on the basis of this equality, we know that social division and hierarchy play important roles in Hinduism, Confucianism, Islam and Roman Catholicism. 'Dignity' is often achieved in these views by striving to fulfil one's particular vocation within an ordered set of roles.

Second view on human rights stress on the requisites for human well-being. Thus, Gewirth (1985) argued that human rights are not just a product of morality but protect the basic freedom and well-being necessary for human agency. He identified three types of rights that address different levels of well-being.[1] Basic rights safeguard one's subsistence or basic well-being. Non-subtractive rights maintain the capacity for fulfilling purposive agency, and additive rights provide the requisites for developing one's capabilities—such as education. This approach has been strongly criticised by some relativists like Douglas Husak[2] as they argue that human rights cannot be universal if they are derived from one's capacity for agency. Another approach on the universality of human rights is based on evolution and human development (O'Manique, 1990).[3] This approach is interested to find a truly universal notion of human rights which is not as susceptible (as is dignity) to the controversy of the relativists. This view is primarily based on the analysis of the basic requisites for survival of individuals as these requisites have an universal character and can be ascertained by scientific inquiry. O'Manique advanced his argument by basing human survival upon the full development of human potential. Thus, according to this view, human rights would include rights to things needed for subsistence but also go on to cover all aspects of intellectual and emotional development. But the basic problem with this view is that the meaning of a fulfilling survival is relative to each culture and individual, and to extend this argument further one may cite examples from some religious beliefs which hold that a person's life can be sacrificed. The fourth and final theoretical approach on human rights has stressed on providing the needs for human existence.[4] Human rights may be limited to providing all humans with the needs for their physical subsistence but this subsistence would involve a certain degree of minimal comfort beyond merely keeping one's organs working. This need-based approach is considered as more acceptable to be applied globally as there is less disagreement over what is 'needed' for, 'survival' than one finds for 'dignity', 'well-being', or 'development'. But relativists argue that different cultures have quite diverse notions of what food, dress, or shelter and even more differences are found in approaches to health care as some societies do not owe allegiance to 'Western' medicine as they have different notions on diseases and cure.

Thus, one can find that the foundations for human rights are not universally accepted. Let me move on to another debatable topic, i.e. 'why (or whether) human rights issues are important for the Third World countries particularly in the backdrop of globalisation?' It is evident that globalisation in its present form has also brought phenomenons like great inequities, mass impoverishment and despair. It has further fractured society along the existing fault lines of class, gender and community while, almost irreversibly, it widens the gap internationally between the rich and the poor nations. Globalisation has resulted in gross human rights violations for millions of workers (particularly women workers), peasants and farmers, and indigenous communities, particularly in the Third World countries.

(a) In Third World, globalisation has resulted in the violation of the fundamental right to work. In their drive for profits, transnational companies, have been restructuring their operations on a global scale.

This has resulted in massive unemployment and underemployment in these countries. Two other major impacts of globalisation are also noticeable which is of fundamental importance in relation to human rights. First, there is an accentuation of the process of informalisation of labour and the growth of the informal economy. Here, not only are the wages low, but also the legal protections of workers are minimal. Second, the 'feminisation of labour' since women constitute the overwhelming majority of labour in the low-wage industries. Workers in such industries are not only inadequately protected as regards health and safety, but they also do not enjoy security of employment in view of the tendency of such investors to move offshore to cut costs. All these cause violations of some essential rights like the right to work and right to health for a huge majority of humanity.

(b) Globalisation also poses a serious threat to the right of livelihood of millions of traditional farmers in the Third World countries. The requirement to comply with the GATT Final Act has opened up the agricultural sector to imports (mainly from the North) and as land laws are revised to facilitate corporate farming, there will inevitably be large-scale displacement of the traditional farmers. All these developments, and in particular the drive under the WTO regime to make access to food mainly dependent upon market mechanisms, are a threat to food security for the Third World countries—the most fundamental of all human rights.

(c) It might further be noted that globalisation has provided a new impetus to the destruction of the habitat and livelihood of indigenous communities in many countries of the Third World. The continuing displacement of such communities as a consequence of the intensification of such economic activities as mining and logging is a grim reminder of such violations of human rights.

(d) IMF and World Bank initiated Structural Adjustment Programs (SAP) as the main mechanism for promoting globalisation and evidences suggest that SAP has resulted in a massive violation of human rights. These programs forcing substantial curtailments of state investments in the essential sectors like health, education, food, housing, infrastructure, etc. had resulted in massive violations of various rights like the right to work, the right to food, the right to adequate housing, the right to health, the right to education and the right to development. Particularly important is the combined effect of the violation of the right to food and the right to health which has had devastating consequences in the Third World.

Thus, one can see why the human rights issues are more important now for the Third World countries in South particularly when the forces of globalisation have created havoc in these countries. With this renewed emphasis on human rights, which was never so pertinent in the history of humanity, new horizons are opening up to incorporate various emerging aspects of human rights particularly in the Third World countries. Agencies (mostly non-government and sometimes government) in these countries as well as the international agencies are now getting more and more active in recording and fighting against these human rights violations. Various research institutes in these countries as well as in the developed world are studying these human rights issues at length. But the debate regarding how the struggle universality in human rights might challenge various forms of cultural diversity and innovation in Third World countries are getting less emphasis till today. But, as anthropological studies indicate, such diversity is huge, ranging from differences in the rights and duties of the individual versus individual obligations and duties to ethnic, cultural, religious or family groups as seen in various traditional Third World countries. Thus, questions may be asked whether the growing expansion of particular human rights norms provides a new discourse by which people can defend the unrepresented or under-represented section of the population. Or is there a way that human rights movements can provide support for local discourses of human rights?

So I argue that we need culturally relative (predominantly non-Western) discourses for the Third World countries which would possibly ensure the protection and promotion of both natural and human rights as well as the cultural diversity in the Third World countries. I also argue that without these discourses, the human right situation in Third World countries would worsen. The reasons for this sort of pessimistic argument are on the one hand, globalisation has virtually unleashed ruthless forces to ensure free movement of capital and resources causing increasing vulnerability in the Third World countries for their citizens as they face more and more human rights violations and on the other hand, the perceived universalism in the human rights approaches is sometimes endangering various forms of cultural diversities and local innovations.

This collection of papers would address some of the issues discussed above. Prof. Buddhadeb Chaudhuri in his article on "Human Security, Indigenous People and Development" (the key address in the seminar) has argued that in spite of every effort from the different agencies to eliminate conflict, inequality and to establish inalienability of human rights the world has not become a safer place and it is least safe for the indigenous and marginalised people. He argued that the very notion of human security could be debated as an attempt by the West to impose its values and political institutions on non-Western societies. There should be non-Western approaches particularly by the Asian thinkers which should cover the rich multicultural and varied historical experiences of Asia. Thus, according to Prof. Chaudhuri, justice, equality and human dignity are inherent in human rights discourses and inextricably related with human security. He further forwarded his argument with the effect of development programmes on the various sections of populations in the Third World countries. While these development programmes have benefited some people it also created disruption and displacement for the others particularly the poor and vulnerable section of the population. Thus, the question of survival and security of a large section of humanity has become also related with the developmental paradigm. Prof. Chaudhuri argued that while exploitation of natural resources cannot be stopped but one can look for sustainable developmental programmes with a genuine participatory approach which is open, accessible and accountable for the security of the larger population.

In his article Prof. Suranjan Das has eloquently presented the basic foundations of human rights as we find the national and international arenas. He observed that there has been a huge gap in the implementation of the covenants of human rights. The reason of such gap, he argued, was due to overemphasising political and civil rights at the expense of social and economic rights. He also argued that without sufficient social and economic capabilities one cannot expect to ensure the protection of all the necessary rights of all the sections of the population. He further discussed on one of the most important debates in the present day human rights situation in India, i.e. the issue of the secessionist forces active in different parts of India and the violation of human rights by both the government as well as those secessionists. His article also explored the dubious human rights records of the US led Western industrialised nations. He argued that on the one hand, these countries are regularly violating human rights in different parts of the world like Iraq, Libya or Afghanistan and on the other hand, they accuse China and India for their alleged violations of human rights. Prof. Das has strongly advocated for a 'holistic' approach to the notion of human rights which he thinks can only be developed under aegis of the progressive and democratic forces in the society.

Prof. Ishita Mukhopadhyay made an important contribution on "The Rights of the Other: Some Questions" in this volume. In her article, she revisited the question of rights of women and the question of inclusion in the domain of human rights and the socio-economic context of these rights. Prof. Mukhopadhyay started her argument by reviewing the question as represented in the existing literatures on human rights. In her article, Prof. Mukhopadhyay also presented the context of violence against women in the history of mankind and she explained that the process of production and reproduction associated with patriarchal structure were primarily responsible for this violence. Thus, Prof. Mukhopadhyay concluded that the issue of women's rights could only be properly explained if it was put in proper perspective, i.e. with the larger socio-economic issues particularly the rights of the deprived in the society.

Prof. Debi Chatterjee's article on "Dalits and Human Rights" primarily deals with the various aspects of marginalisation of the Dalit population right from the inception of Brahminical form of Hinduism to the present-day globalisation. The essay also goes through the various forms of Dalit resistance movements particularly from 1990s like National Campaign on Dalit Human Rights (NCDHR). Prof. Chatterjee also described the importance of formal meetings in the form of National Conference of Dalit Organisations (NACDOR) in 2001 and 2006 in deliberating the issues related to the rights of Dalits. Prof. Chatterjee also discussed on the role of United Nations in this regard. She reckoned that the World Conference against Racism, Racial Discrimination, Xenophobia and Related Intolerance (WCAR), held under the umbrella of United Nations in Durban, South Africa, 2001 was also a milestone in this regard as the WCAR recognised the caste-based discrimination as an important issue and various organisations in that conference criticised the role of the Indian government in preventing this discrimination. Lastly Prof. Chatterjee stressed on the need for a holistic, integrated human rights perspective to properly deal with the question of Dalit rights.

Dr. Siddhartha Guha Ray in his article on the "Civil Rights in India: Towards Framing a Contemporary History" has critically reviewed the history of civil rights in India. Dr. Guha Ray argued that even after the colonial rule the ruling party in the Centre has adopted innumerable measures which are detrimental to civil liberties and human rights of the Indian citizen despite the constitution of the independent India which guarantees the fundamental rights of the Indian citizens. The constituent assembly in 1950 passed one such act Preventive Detention Act under the leadership of Sardar Ballabhbhai Patel which has been widely misused. Other such black Acts in the independent India include Defence of India Rules (DIR) passed in 1962 during the Sino-Indian War, Maintenance of Internal Security Act (MISA) passed in 1971 ostensibly to fight naxalite movement, Code of Criminal Procedure (Amendment) Act passed by the Janata Government in 1977, Terrorist and Disruptive Activities Act (TADA) passed by the Rajiv Gandhi government to fight terrorism in Kashmir, Punjab and North Eastern states though this Act has also been used against the minorities in various parts of the India, and Armed Forces (Special Power) Act (AFSPA) which was passed much earlier in 1958 and has been misused extensively particularly in the North Eastern states.

Dr. A.K. Ghosh in his article "Environment and Human Rights" argued that the environmental concern has been back-seated by developmental activities from 20th century. This trend has increased with globalisation as it advocates for privatization leading to the shift of common pool of resources to the private operators. But a global consensus on the need of sustainable models of development has prevented further downgrading of the environmental concerns. Dr. Ghosh also emphasised the role of public awareness on the right to land, clean water, air and forest in establishing human rights over environment. Dr. Ghosh also discussed on the changing perception of development where more participatory approaches are being increasingly explored by the planners and policy-makers.

Prof. Sumita Sen in her article "Ensuring Human Rights for Refugees" discussed on different aspects of human rights for refugees as she stressed the need for adopting different categories of people viz. refugees, IDPs, stateless, illegal migrants, etc. She reckoned that most of the refugees are now from Africa and Asia and the respective states responded in different ways in dealing with these refugee situations. In most cases, lack of any or adequate legislation of the respective countries on refugees and other such groups have only worsened situations. Prof. Sen further stressed on the need of a comprehensive and well-equipped approach having a transnational applicability as it would ensure the prevention of mass exodus from a country as well as effective handling of the refugees in terms of their repatriation as well as rehabilitation.

In his article on "Science, War and Human Rights", Prof. Syamal Chakrabarti has argued that in the history of mankind various rights and privileges of people have been denied during the time of war. He further argued that during the time of war the ruling elites have always wanted that the entire population of the country be driven by a bigotry of nationalism. In the history of mankind some scientists have become the victim of these chauvinisms and acted according to the will of ruling elites. However, Prof. Chakrabarti argued, some scientists could overcome these all-embracing bigotry and worked for the benefit of mankind. He further stated that the two World Wars at an interval of 25 years bore the testimony of human genocide and a complete denial of human rights at a massive scale. Both the wars ended but the ideology of aggression and domination remained unabated on the surface of earth.

Tathagata Chakraborty, in his article "Problems of Human Rights as Reflected in Folk Literature of Bengal: Focus on Folk Songs in Particular" discussed on the elements found in the folk literature of Bengal. He took a segment of Bengali folk literature (viz. folk tales, proverbs and adages, vows, ballads and folk-songs) as his point of departure for this purpose. He showed how these elements in Bengali folk literature reflect concerns over various aspects of human rights: the right to life and liberty, freedom of thought and expression and equality before the law. He further argued that though they might appear innocuous, a careful observation might bring out their concerns over various social issues related to human rights like the problem of dowry, child marriage, the agony of an unhappy marriage, the bondage of women, persecution by the mother-in-law, sister-in-law or the husband, economic exploitation in various forms.

In their article "The Ways of Dying in Retrospect: A Study on Care for and Rights to Live", Suman Nath, Priyadarsini Sengupta and Dr. Gopalkrishna Chakraborti presented a comparative experience with patients 'being' in terminal illness. Two different field experiences were explored in that article, viz. field interactions at one suburban cancer hospital and internet chatting with people from 'first world' countries. The application of a phenomenological paradigm showed an alternative way of treating and studying such a delicate field like terminal illness. With a brief overview of existing literature the paper incorporated human rights, health issues, philosophical understandings and methodological suggestions. With a co-constructive approach the paper instigated some serious human right issues related to 'aided' ways of living rather than dying with economic and mental burden in a broader sense of care and positive attitude of life.

Dr. Subir Biswas and Ganesh Chandra Mallick in their article "Declining Sex Ratio: The Question to Right to Born and to Live (A Study among Rajbansis of a Village in Darjeeling District, West Bengal)" argued that the sex ratio of human group not only depends upon biological factors but also upon cultural factors. They argued that though the biologically vulnerable nature of the boys make the sex ratio in favour of girls in developing and underdeveloped countries the sex ratio declines rapidly favouring males due to various socio-cultural factors. In their empirical study on the Rajbansi population in the village Rangia near Siliguri town they tried to identify these socio-cultural factors.

Arpita Ghosh and Ahana Datta Mukherjee in their article "Protection of Child Rights: Concern, Issues and Reality" stressed the need for the recognition of child rights as one of the basic human rights and highlighted the need of human rights education in schools for both the children and the trainers. Ankita Ghosh in her article on Right to Information (RTI) argued that RTI has been a powerful instrument for making participatory development throughout the world as it has made the administrative authorities and the elected representatives work according to their policies and/or principles. She also argued that the Right to Information Act passed in the Indian Parliament in 2005 would go a long way in making the development participatory. Dr. S.K. Nandy and Dr. D.K. Adak in their article "Rights and Privileges in India: An Overview" emphasized the perspectives of rights and privileges among the children, women and older members of our society in India. They also argued that the absence of rights and privileges prevent different sections of the population get properly integrated often leading to anguish, eruption of violence, conflicts, etc. Prasenjit Sarkar contributed on "Human Rights: The Indian Experience" where he argued that from the time of antiquity, India witnessed many upheavals against the violation of natural and civil rights sometimes forcing the authorities to mend their ways. All these experiences facilitated India to achieve the present state of democracy.

Dr. T.R. Maruthi in his article "International Human Rights Law" went through various information relating to human rights and its different facets with international humanitarian law, terrorism, regionalism, and postmodernism. He further extended his observation on the ways of improving international human rights by the ratification of international human rights instruments; enhancement of enforcement mechanisms; measures for effective national implementation; respect for human rights by parties to the conflict; dissemination of conventions; enactment of penal legislations; and translation of treaties into national languages.

In her paper "Adam, Eve and 'Others'—Analyzing the Right to Survive with Dignity of Third Sex in India" Dr. Lopamudra Sengupta highlighted the pain and misery faced by the Hijras in India for decades. In doing so, the author questioned the dominant norms and practices of the society that robbed mankind from human essentialism and reduced them to objects of non-entity. By addressing the questions of gender inequality, the paper focuses on the fact that no human rights can be achieved in the society unless the "homophobia" ceases to exist. The paper sought to find solution within the human rights framework.

With this brief note on the contributions, I would like to state that this collection of articles should be regarded as a modest attempt to accommodate some of the expanding horizons of human rights. This collection could not accommodate many other aspects of the burgeoning fields of human rights which might be done by this editor in a future project. It is expected that this collection will be an useful one for the scholars, teachers and the students of human rights.

## REFERENCES

Gewirth, Alan. 1985. *Are There any Absolute Rights? Theories of Rights.* New York: Oxford University Press.

O'Manique, John. 1990. "Universal and Inalienable Human Rights: A Search for Foundations." *Human Rights Quarterly,* 465-85.

## NOTES

1. Allan Gewirth, "Why There Are Human Rights" (1985), 11, *Social Theory and Practice*, 235-48.
2. Douglas Husak, "Why There Are No Human Rights" (1984), 10, *Social Theory and Practice*, 125-41.
3. John O'Manique, "Universal and Inalienable Human Rights: A Search for Foundations" (1990), 12, *Human Rights Quarterly,* 465-85.
4. A more recent needs-based approach to human rights is found in: Johan Galtung, *Human Rights in Another Key*, Cammbridge, Mass: Polity Press, 1994.

# Human Security, Indigenous People and Development

2

*Buddhadeb Chaudhuri*

## Introduction

The Universal Declaration of Human Rights adopted around fifty-eight years back was a great step to eliminate conflict and establish equal and inalienable rights of all members of the human society, rich or poor, regardless of status, race, religion, colour, sex or political background. Nevertheless, the world has seen barbarous inhumanity during the two world wars. Prof. René Cassin, the noted French jurist, who was connected with this Declaration, was offered the Nobel Prize after 20 years in 1968. Once he said, 'Men are not always good'.

In the evolution of human rights, the Western powers were more interested to give priority to the Civil and Political Rights, often referred as 'First Generation Rights', while the Socialist countries were interested in the Economic, Social and Cultural Rights, often referred as 'Second Generation Rights'. The concept of 'Third Generation Rights' was introduced afterwards to refer the rights of the people or groups including right to Self-Determination, Development and Environment. The Vienna World Conference on Human Rights, 1993 reaffirmed that the civil, political, economic, social and cultural rights are 'universal, interdependent and indivisible'. It has been observed that:

> Human Rights are best understood as part of law, part of philosophy and part of political movement. The values which drive the idea of human rights owe almost as much to poetry and music as they do to legal principles. They owe nearly as much to the spirituality of all the great religions and to the eternal quest for righteousness as they

> do to revolutions and the demand for freedom from state tyranny.... The idea of rights has changed over time because people have acted together to claim rights in different circumstances and with varying goals in mind.... In other words, in the history of humans, distinct periods arrive when new rights come into prominence as a force of change. That does not make Economic, Social and Cultural Rights and other rights any way less important than Civil and Political Rights.

It is really interesting to note the contribution of the International Human Rights regime in the last few decades. The development has profound impact on conceptual and practical issues. In international law, the sovereign states were the main subject and actors. The international human rights regime has projected on the centre-stage the individual. This has interesting implications in the context of the scope of human rights and human security.

Let me start provide certain facts of the 20th century. In this period, some 100 million people were killed in armed conflicts and further 120 million dead as a result of politically related violence where religion or race or ethnicity or political background was the main factor.

- At the start of the century, during armed conflict, 5 per cent of the casualties were civilians, at the end of the century, 90 per cent of such casualties were civilians.
- Over 120 million land mines were deployed in more than 64 countries and most of the victims were civilians (Venkatachaliah, 2002).

The concept of 'human security' has initiated the debate—what 'security' means and how to achieve it. The concept has been defined and pursued in different ways by different nation states: as a means of reducing the human costs of violent conflicts, as a strategy to enable governments to address basic human needs and offset the inequities of globalization, and as a means to provide social safety nets to impoverished, marginalized people. The discussion on the disarmament-development nexus that took place in various UN forums in response to the Cold War arms race contributed in the understanding of human security. Besides, a number of commissions like the Brandt Commission, the Bruntland Commission and the Commission on Global Governance helped to change the focus of security analysis from national and state security to security of the people. In fact, subsequently there was a growing recognition of non-military threats in the global security debate. The Human Development Report of UNDP (1994) provided seven separate components of human security:

1. Economic security (assured basic income);
2. Food security (physical and economic access to food);
3. Health security (relative freedom from disease and infection);
4. Environmental security (access to safe water, clean air and a non-degraded land system);
5. Personal security (security from physical violence and threats);
6. Community security (security of cultural identity); and
7. Political security (enjoyment of basic human rights and freedom).

Some have criticized the above scope and definition of human security as too broad. However, others feel that a broader definition is necessary and desirable considering the wider constituency of UN. Some other definitions are more explicitly linked to human rights and humanitarian law. This marked a shift in the norms of state sovereignty with particular reference to human rights protection. Canada criticized the scope of human security as provided by UNDP for focussing more on underdevelopment and ignoring human security resulting from violent conflict (DFAIT, 1999). The varied notions and concepts of human security initiated an interesting debate in the context of national security and human security and 'freedom from want' and 'freedom from fear'. It is interesting to note that some Asian thinkers and governments see human security as yet another attempt by the West to impose its values and political institutions on non-Western societies. Others have pointed out the non-military threats to human security as a reality in many countries and emphasized the need of a collective human security agenda. Canada focussed human security as 'security of the people' which was also supported by Norway. The two countries have formed a Human Security Partnership identifying a nine-point agenda of human security covering:

> land-mines, formation of an International Criminal Court, human rights, international humanitarian law, women and children in armed conflict, small arms proliferation, child soldiers, child labour and northern cooperation.

The observation of Japan in the context of the perception of human security may be mentioned here:

> In Japan's view, however, human security is a much broader concept. We believe that freedom from want is no less critical than freedom from fear. So long as its objectives are to ensure the survival and dignity of individuals as human beings, it is necessary to go beyond thinking of human security solely in terms of protecting human life in conflict situations. (Chapman, 1983)

To understand human security, Astrid Suhrke (1999) emphasized the issue of 'vulnerability' with reference to three categories of victims: those of war and internal conflicts, those living at or below subsistence levels, and victims of natural disaster. Dr. Sverre Lodgaard (2000) of the Norwegian Institute of International Affairs advocated a narrower scope of human security which he felt should not be mixed up with human development. Thus, the debate of human security arises from varied perceptions: the Western usage reflects the individualistic ethos of liberal democracy which conflicts with the Asian approach to human rights which, as felt by Asian thinkers should cover the different cultural contexts and historical experiences of Asia. Human security calls for a shift of security considering from state security to security of the people, which includes both individuals and communities considering the survival and well-being of all communities. The observation of Prof. Amartya Sen (1999), a Nobel Laureate and a Member of International Commission on Human Security, is worth mentioning here. He pointed out the crucial link between freedom from fear and freedom from want. Human security gives emphasis on human dignity without ignoring the rights of societies and non-political rights. Safety and dignity of individuals or people cannot be compromised. In fact, in the human security paradigm, the tolerance of human rights violation for economic development or social stability is not acceptable.

## Democracy and Human Security

In the last twenty years alone 81 more countries of the world have moved towards democratic practices, some 33 of them had their military regimes replaced by civil governments. Democratic governance and human development have an intimate inter-relationship. Participatory decisions are at the heart of human development. Authoritarian regimes often argue that they have advantages in building strong states that can make tough decisions in the interests of people. They also argue that democratic processes create disorder and impede efficient management—'that countries must choose between democracy and development, between extending political freedom and expanding incomes'. The Human Development Report, 2002, however, provided the opposite picture:

> .... There are good reasons to believe that democracy and growth are compatible. With just two exceptions, all of the world's richest countries—those with per capita income of more than $20,000 (in 2000 purchasing power parity) —have the world's most democratic regimes. In addition, 42 of the 48 high human development countries are democracies.... A systematic study by Adam Prezeworski and others of 135 countries from 1950-90 discredits the notion of a trade off between democracy and development. (Human Development Report, 2002)

It has been further noted that democracies are better than authoritarian regimes in managing conflicts and catastrophes. Democracy provides for political space and institutional mechanisms for debate and change, particularly in managing sudden turn downs that threaten human survival. The Human Development Report says:

.... In India famines were common under colonial rule—for example 2 to 3 million people died in 1943 Bengal famine. But since independence and democratic rule, there has been no recurrence of famine—despite severe crop failures and massive losses of purchasing power for large segments of population as in 1968, 1973, 1979 and 1987. Each time the government acted to avoid famine. Food production fell largely in 1973 during drought in Maharashtra, but famine was averted partly because 5 million people were put to work in public works projects.... (Human Development Report, 2002)

Justice, equality and human dignity are the watchwords of human rights discourse. But the inequity of the international economic order has produced unacceptable levels of inequality, both internally and internationally. In the USA (1994) itself the poorest quintile of the population had 1.5 per cent of income and consumption while the top quintile had 45.2 per cent. This reflects, in a non-trivial sense, the anomalies and inequities of the international economic order. Inequality between and amongst countries has also increased. The income gap between the fifth of the world's people living in the richest countries and the fifth in the poorest was 74 to 1 in 1997, up from 60 to 1 in 1990 and 30 to 1 in 1960 (World Development Report, 1999). Over the 30 years from 1960 to 1990 the affluent 20 per cent of the world have enhanced their share of incomes and consumption from 70.1 per cent to 86 per cent while the poorest 20 per cent have had their share reduced to 1 per cent. This is the manifestation of a growth, which is ruthless, rootless, voiceless, jobless, and futureless.

By the late 1990s, the fifth of the world's people living in highest-income countries had:

- 86% of world GDP—the bottom fifth just 1%.
- 82% of world export markets—the bottom fifth just 1%.
- 68% of foreign direct investment—the bottom fifth had just 1%.

- 74% of world telephone lines, today's basic means of communication—the bottom fifth just 1.5%.
- Income of the richest 5% of the world is 114 times that of the poorest 5%.
- Richest 1% has as much income as the poorest 57%.
- In more personal terms, just three richest men, Bill Gates, Warren Buffet and Paul Allen, have wealth equal to the income of 48 poor countries, consisting of over a billion people.

Since independence India has made some impressive achievements. Particularly significant has been the increase in agricultural production. Between 1950 and 2000, the index of agricultural production increased more than fourfold. Between 1960 and 2000 wheat production went up from 11 million tonnes to 75.6 million tonnes and the production of rice increased from 35 million tonnes to 89.5 million tonnes. This is no mean achievement for a country that relied on food aid until the middle of the 1960s. The rosy picture of the success of the green revolution is generally projected. It is true that the production has increased considerably, but it has also increased inequality. The rich have become richer and the poor poorer. Again, one may notice the many cases of suicide committed by the farmers in different parts of India. As 'modern' agriculture needs more investment, the farmers often are forced to take loan for agriculture and if they do not get the proper return, often they commit suicide, reflecting the increasing insecurity of human being.

The most significant is population growth. Kerala has a fertility rate of 1.7, which is equal to that of Britain and France, is below 1.9 of China and 2.0 of the U.S.A. This according to Prof. Amartya Sen has been achieved:

> ...with no coercion, but mainly through the emergence of new values—a process in which political and social dialogues have played a major part. The level of literacy in Kerala, especially the female literacy, is higher than that of every province in China. This has greatly

> contributed to making informed social and political dialogues possible. (Sen, 1999)

In India life expectancy was just 20.9 years in 1910. In 2000, the life expectancy of the urban female in Kerala went up to 80 years. There is abundant empirical evidence of the inter-link between the spread of education and economic achievement.

> The lack of education is one of the major reasons for their unequal status of women in society. Denial of access to organized knowledge to women from ancient times has contributed to the increasing subordination of women. (Sen, 1999)

Maternal anaemia in India is about 57 per cent. It is nearly 71 per cent for the Dalits and underprivileged sections. An international comparison of infant mortality and maternal mortality rates are given below:

| Country | Maternal mortality (per lakh birth) | Infant mortality rate – per 1000 births | Births attended by skilled health staff | No. of women getting prenatal care |
|---|---|---|---|---|
| UK | 7 | 6 | 98% | 92% |
| USA | 8 | 7 | 99% | 94% |
| China | 60 | 32 | 78% | 79% |
| India | 410 | 69 | 42% | 60% |

Within Indian society itself the intra-societal and inter-regional imbalances are significant. While the infant mortality rate in urban Kerala is about 12, it is still as high as 146 in Kishangunj in Bihar. One Human Development Report (UNDP) said that a child born in Kerala today can expect to live longer than one born in Washington. The percentage of child births under skilled health staff is 93 per cent in Kerala and 3 per cent in Uttar Pradesh.

The UNDP report of 1994 made a very interesting observation. In the developing countries nearly 65 per cent of the diseases could have been eliminated if we could provide safe drinking water. Unfortunately, it is not happening.

The main issues of human rights in many countries are education, prevalence of maternal anaemia, low birth-weight related neurological deficiencies, children's education, particularly of the girl child. Poverty is, of course, the worst and most crucial human rights deprivation.

Even in 1994, the Human Development Report of 1994, in its chapter 'New Dimensions of Human Security' had said:

> Fifty years ago, Albert Einstein summed up the discovery of atomic energy with characteristic simplicity: 'Everything changed'. He went on to predict: 'we shall require a substantially new manner of thinking if mankind is to survive'. But five decades later we need another profound transition in thinking—from nuclear security to human security. (Human Development Report, 1994)

The report changed the concept of security from its earlier narrow connotation and attached it to the legitimate concerns of ordinary people who sought security in daily lives.

> For many of them, security symbolizes protection from the threat of disease, hunger, political repression and environmental hazards. With the dark shadows of the cold war receding, one can now see that conflicts are within nations rather than between nations. For most people, feeling of insecurity arises more from worries about daily life than from the dread of a cataclysmic world event. Will they and their families have enough to eat? Will they lose their jobs? Will their streets and neighbourhoods safe from crime? Will they be tortured by repressive state? Will they become victim of violence because of their gender? Will their religion or ethnic origin target them for persecution. (Human Development Report, 1994)

The U.N. Secretary General, in his millennium report said:

> The century just ended was disfigured, time and again, by ruthless conflict.... Grinding poverty and striking inequality persist within and among countries even amidst unprecedented wealth. Diseases, old and new, threaten to undo painstaking progress. Nature's life-sustaining services, on which our species depends for its survival, are being seriously disrupted and degraded by our own everyday activities. (UN Millennium Report, 1995)

A number of development programmes have been initiated which have varied effect on population. In many places, the development programmes have benefited some while created disruption and displacement for others. Displacement of a larger population mostly illiterate and unorganized weaker section in the context of development of the region or nation is very common in most of the countries in Asia, Africa and Latin America. Since there is displacement of a large section of population, the access and command over natural resources are affected, the survival and security of the people are also affected. One cannot stop exploitation of natural resources but what one is now looking for is how to achieve sustainable development. This may demand a new development strategy with a genuine participatory approach and creating a process of natural resource use which is open, accessible and accountable for the security of the larger population. In fact development is expected to improve the quality of life which is not possible when security is affected for a sizable section of the population. Development may be considered as those changes which are required, but have minimum disruptive effects on the concerned population. The protest of the people in the context of different so-called development projects in different parts of the world or many forest development programmes raises a very fundamental question, the development does not start with goods, it starts with people. Again, globalization has created new opportunities and problems. Prof. Amartya Sen has noted that global participation is basically an enhancement of economic opportunity and its costs can be minimized through appropriate domestic policies, paying particular attention to the availability and distributional equity of economic and social opportunities. He also stressed the importance of certain positive social changes in this regard like land reforms, spread of education, better health care, freedom of work and freedom of fear, which are very much related to human security. He also observed, 'these are not much the social consequences of economic reforms, but the economic consequences of social reforms. The market economy flourishes on the foundations of social development—a lesson which India has yet to learn' (Sen, 1999).

The Commission on Global Governance distinguished between the security of state and security of people. Because of emerging socio-economic and political situation, the security of the people is very much affected. After the publication of the Commission Report in 1994, efforts have been made to define the security of people, the human security, more rigorously, along with practical ways of promoting it. Thus, human security means the security of people: their physical safety, socio-economic well-being, protection of human rights and freedom. The fundamental components of human security are the security of people against threats to life, health, livelihood, personal safety and human dignity. Naturally, the concerned socio-economic and political systems play a very crucial role in the context of human security and its protection.

## Environment, Development and Human Security

The world today is deeply concerned with ecological issues. Man for his ever-growing needs uses resources in nature. In this way he promotes development. The use of natural resources and the initiation of development produce changes in ecology. The nature of changes in ecology manifests the character of development. The character of development, again, determines the use of resources. The pattern of use of resources reflects to a certain extent the path of development that a governing group has decided to follow. Although the issues have to be analyzed from different points of view, the role of human being as an agent of change has to be taken as focal point. In the relationship between development and environment, adjustment is the need, but conflict is generally the outcome. Industrial, agricultural and infrastructural developments have created many environmental problems due to misunderstanding of the system in nature. In the planning model, the environmental issues were not adequately considered in the past. This is now regarded as too costly to be avoided. The process of planning and concomitant administrative decisions should attach top priority to the resolution of the contradiction between development and environment.

Immediately after the colonial rule in many countries there was an acute shortage of food for which the government of the concerned country desperately tried to increase food production at any cost. Maybe an increase or growth in production was the goal at that moment and maybe the objective was achieved in a given context, but is it possible to equate it with development? Any increase in production is growth but development is a broader and wider term and it has other connotations too. It not only includes growth, but an equitable distribution of facilities and resources and reduction, if not elimination, of exploitative practices are also implied. Of late, another very important and crucial indicator has also been added to it. It is the question of environment. Man, for his ever-growing needs, uses resources in nature. The use of natural resources and initiation of development produce changes in ecology. In the relationship between development and environment, adjustment is the need. Any activity is likely to produce some changes in ecology, but it is to be seen how these activities are affecting the ecology. Any activity adversely affecting the ecology cannot be considered as development. Thus, development includes both qualitative and quantitative changes—it improves the socio-economic condition and also quality of life of the majority population of the concerned society without adversely affecting the environment and thus not creating any problem for other groups or communities directly not involved in the activity. It thus helps to exploit the natural resources in a better way without any grave adverse environmental consequence.

Development of any region has three main dimensions, economic, social and environmental, and none of these dimensions can be neglected if the real development of a region is to be achieved. Of all the three, the environmental dimension is all pervasive, but it has been hitherto neglected. During the last couple of years a wave to protect the environment is blowing everywhere. The potential environmental damage, the magnitude of the waste management problems are directly related to the growth of economic activities which demands some regions to reduce the rate of economic growth resulting in regional imbalances. On the other hand, a reduction of economic growth rate would lead to unemployment, poverty and several other social problems.

Economic activities always generate residuals and release them into the common property resources of air, water and land. They create external discomfort for the society, which resides there. However, there are strong moral and ethical justifications for not imposing such costs and injuries upon the region and the society. But, the internation of the externalities is virtually impossible in the case of large-scale production by the use of technology without proper policy to manage the environment. Though the principle of permitting optimal levels of emissions and environmental damages in every region for every economic activity sounds as a better rule to be followed in the regional development programme, it has to pay for the environmental damage in the long-run. Hence, the scale of regional development should be comprehensive enough to manage the environmental damage.

Other sets of social and political problems need to be examined. That what is regarded as an enormous ecological problem by one social group, may be regarded by another as an economic opportunity with negligible external costs. A sparsely populated region having large assimilative capacities in its air and water resources may appear to other regions or the nation as an ideal dumping ground of residuals which may be highly objectionable and unfair for the receiving region. It is also to be noted that the residents of well-developed region expects the residents of underdeveloped region to forego the benefit of regional economic development so that the residents of a well-developed region may have external economics of non-polluted vacation areas as second homes in the countryside.

Industrialized regions and nations have already started protecting their environment at the cost of other regions and environments by making heavy demands upon the existing limited stocks of non-renewable minerals, metals, fuels, and other natural resources. Some of the Third World countries find it difficult to take up costly protecting devices to save environment.

Development programmes initiated in tribal-dominated areas often adversely affected the tribal way of life, economy and habitat resulting displacement. This was frequently followed by the encroachment on traditional tribal areas by non-tribals and as the exploitation of natural resources became more intense, it generally affected the ecosystem of the tribal areas. There are the inevitable difficulties of development policy in a situation where the component programmes are funded by international agencies and often supervised by them. Quite often greater emphasis and attention are given to the interests of the developed sectors of the country, such as the industrial sector or the dominant section of the concerned country. The rights and interests of the so-called backward tribals are often treated as being of secondary importance. Actually with the formation of new nation states and increase in population, the exploitation of natural resources becomes more intense and there is tremendous competition to have access and command over natural resources and this often creates conflicts and tension at different levels. The developed countries or rather the multi-national organizations try to control the resources of the less-developed countries, while the dominant sections of the developing countries try to manipulate in such a way that they can enjoy the major share of the national natural resources often depriving the local population, mostly the tribals.

If we take the case of forest, there is no doubt that there is considerable degradation. Thus, people, mostly the women, as they are primarily involved in the collection, are struggling more but getting less. This struggle is directly linked with the level of degradation of forest; where the forest is more degraded, people are forced to struggle more, where it is less degraded, the struggle is much less.

There has been significant land alienation, deforestation and mindless mining operations and other construction activities for the sake of the defence establishments, all leading to displacement and great human misery. Unfortunately, many of these activities were undertaken in the name of development or 'national' interest. Quite often the project-affected people neither received adequate compensation nor resettlement support and little or no benefit out of these activities which greatly and adversely affected their life. The rationale of the 'national interest' to initiate these projects naturally needs thorough review and serious rethinking.

One cannot stop the exploitation of natural resources but what one is now looking for is how to achieve sustainable development. The traditional models of resource use may have an answer to this question. This may demand a new development strategy with a genuine participatory approach and creating a process of natural resource use, which is open, accessible and accountable by devolving power from the state to the local communities in the context of controlling the forest resources.

## Conclusion

With increasing globalization, the exploitation of natural resources all over the world has become more intense often affecting the environment and the interests of the local people predominantly the indigenous people. Their access and command over natural resources are often denied affecting their life support systems. With the formation of new nation states after the colonial rule, large-scale migration and movement of people have also been noted due to socio-political reasons. Now one may find a large number of displaced persons, the refugees or stateless population all over the world, where human rights violations are very common and human security is a major problem.

## REFERENCES

Acharya, Amitava (2002) 'Debating Human Security: East versus the West.' *Islamic Millennium,* 2(3-4): 21-38.

Chapman, J.W.M. and I.T.M. Gow (1983) *Japan's Quest for Comprehensive Security*. London: Frances Printer.

Chaudhuri, Buddhadeb (1991) 'Forest, Forest Development and Community Participation.' *Indian Anthropologist,* 21(1): 9-19.

—— (1997) Development Environment and Forest—Conflict of Commercial and People's Interests: A Cross-cultural Study (A study on India and Malaysia). IDPAD Project Report. New Delhi: ICSSR.

—— (2007) 'Human Security, Human Rights and Development.' In: B. Chaudhuri and S. Chaudhuri (eds.), *Anthropology and human rights in contemporary era*, pp. 408-19, New Delhi: Inter India Publications.

Chaudhuri, Buddhadeb and A.K. Maiti (eds.) (1989) *Forest and Forest Development in India*. New Delhi: Inter India Publications.

Dewitt, David B. and Amitava Acharya (1996) Cooperative Security and Development Assistance: The Relationship between Security and

Development with Reference to Eastern Asia. Eastern Asia Policy Paper, No. 16. Toronto: Joint Centre for Asia Pacific Studies.

Fernandes, Walter and E. Ganguly Thukral (1989) *Development, Displacement and Rehabilitation.* New Delhi: Indian Social Institute.

Gadgil, Madhav and Ramachandra Guha (1995) *Ecology and Equity.* London: Routledge.

Gadgil, Madhav, S. Narendra Prasad and Rauf Ali (1983) 'Forest Management and Forest policy in India: A Critical Review'. In: Walter Fernandes (ed.), *Forest, Environment and People,* New Delhi: Indian Social Institute.

Ganguly, Thukral Enakshi (1992) *Big Dams, Displaced Persons: Rivers of Sorrow, Rivers of Change.* New Delhi: Sage Publications.

Guha, Ramachandra (ed.) (1994) *Social Ecology.* New Delhi: Oxford University Press.

—— (1989) *The Unquiet Woods: Ecological Change and Peasant Resistance in the Himalaya.* New Delhi: Oxford University Press.

—— (1997) 'Social Ecological Research in India: A Status Report'. *Economic and Political Weekly,* 15 February.

Haq, Mahbubul (1994) New Imperatives of Human Security. RGICS Paper No. 17. New Delhi: Rajiv Gandhi Institute of Contemporary Studies.

Hassan, M.J. (1996) 'The Concept of Comprehensive Security'. In: M.J. Hassan and T. Ramnath (eds.), *Conceptualising Asia-Pacific security,* Kuala Lumpur: Institute of Strategic and International Studies.

Lodgaard, Sverre (2000) Human Security: Concept and Operationalization, Paper presented to the Seminar on Human Rights and Peace, Geneva, 8-9 December 2000.

Sen, Amartya (1999) *Development as Freedom.* New York: Knopf.

Suhrke, Astrid (1999) 'Human Security and Security Dialogue Interests of States'. 30(3).

Tehranian, Majid (2002) 'Cultural Security and Global Governance: International Migration and Negotiations of Identity'. *Islamic Millennium,* 2(3-4): 1-20.

United Nations Development Programme (1995) 'Redefining Security: The Human Dimensions'. *Current History,* 94(May): 229-36.

Venkatachaliah, M.N. (2002) Democracy, Human Security and Development, Special Lecture by Former Chief Justice of India and Chairperson, NHRC, at West Bengal State Human Rights Commission on Human Rights Day, 10 December 2002.

# Some Thoughts on Human Rights

3

*Suranjan Das*

Dr. Jyotiprakas Haldar (Principal, Bangabasi Evening College and the Chairman of the session), Dr. Pradip Kr. Ghosh (Principal, Bangabasi College), Dr. Chittabrata Chakraborty (Principal, Bangabasi Morning College), Dr. Subrata Sankar Bagchi (Convenor of the Seminar), Prof. Buddhadeb Chaudhuri (Dr. B.R. Ambedkar Chair Professor), my esteemed colleagues from this college, from other colleges and from other educational institutions, and of course, my very dear students. Could I first put on record my sincere thanks to the college for enabling me to be here? Could I also congratulate the organisers of the seminar for choosing a theme which is a crucial significance not only for the local and national level, but also for the international level?

I shall take only a couple of minutes to proceed from a point where my previous speaker ended. My previous speaker rightly pointed to the importance of visualising a notion of human rights from a holistic standpoint. In that context I would like to submit before you few points for considerations, some of which will surely be addressed during the deliberations of this two day seminar.

The Universal Declaration on Human Rights of the United Nations on 10 December 1948, defined human rights "as a common standard of achievement for all people and for all nations". As Prof. Haldar indicated, this notion of human rights contains two essential ingredients. First, in a way human rights are certain inalienable and inherent rights which are due to men and women as members of society. These are essentially, what I would call, "moral rights" to be guaranteed to each individual of society. Secondly, there are certain legal rights which are to be enforced by law-enforcing agencies. As I see it, while the first set of rights are essentially civil and political rights, the second category of rights are economic, social and cultural rights. Being a signatory to the Universal Declaration of Human Rights, the Indian State has adopted certain constitutional provisions for the implementation of these rights, the latest being the establishment of National Human Rights Commission and the State Human Rights Commissions.

But the question which I would like to pose before you is to what extent the covenants of human rights at the national or international level have been realised in practice. Unfortunately, as I see it, when we look back at the past 60 years, we can notice significant gaps between theory and practice in the realm of human rights. This gap has largely occurred because there has been a tendency to stress political and civil rights at the expense of social and economic rights. Consequently, there has been the degeneration of certain sets of freedoms which have been enumerated as fundamentals of human rights into freedoms, that can be enjoyed only by the economically powerful social groups.

I propose to cite certain examples from India itself. Our constitution enshrines the right to equality before law. But our legal system is such that to ensure protection from law you require substantial economic power. Unless you have basic economic power you cannot fight a case either at the District Court or at the High Court or at the Supreme Court. The right to equality before law has thus become a myth for a vast multitude of people who do not have enough access to economic power. Again, take the case of right to property, considered an inalienable human right. While this right has to be a fundamental right for the propertied classes, it is meaningless to the vast multitude of the Indian masses who do not own property. Besides, in India we are now rightly talking of an environmental regime for maintaining ecological balance. But I submit before you an issue. Now, the cutting down of trees is an offence under the environmental regime. But there may a group of contractors who are felling trees to be used for commercial purpose, and there may be certain tribal groups who are cutting down trees for the purpose of fuel. The question that I pose is: can we treat both these cases on the same platform? As I see it, this cannot be done.

What I am trying to argue is that countries—including our country—which have bourgeois democratic constitutions and which do not recognise either the right to work or the freedom from economic exploitation as an inalienable right, human rights, have unfortunately degenerated to a set of rights that are usually enjoyed by the economically and socially powerful groups. Unless a person has a guaranteed employment and enjoys basic means of subsistence, and unless a person is guaranteed freedom from poverty, all other rights of freedom become abstract principles for him or her. In fact, many of the Western democratic States, have been violators of some of the basic human rights. For example, still now in some of the European countries there is no right to equal pay for both the sexes. Racial discrimination is a living reality in many of the European countries. Even in the USA, which prides itself as a country at the forefront in promoting human rights, the Blacks and the Whites do not in actual reality enjoy the same human rights.

I do feel that unless there is a telescoping of political and socio-economic rights, human rights cannot be a reality for the majority section in a society, whether in a Western democratic State or in a Third World State like India. We often forget that the Soviet leadership alone realised this indispensability of telescoping political and socio-economic rights, and it was because of the Soviet insistence that the United Nations enacted a separate covenant for economic and cultural rights. But unfortunately, in the context of the decline of the Soviet bloc, and the consequent victory of imperialist dominated globalisation, there has been the virtual non-enactment of this particular covenant.

Nevertheless, we have to recognise the crucial importance of human rights in developing and sustaining a democratic polity. India adopted a federal and democratic constitution, in the aftermath of her independence. But much of the fundamental rights enshrined in the constitution remains inaccessible to the majority section of the society. And, I am sure that this seminar will deliberate on how we can make these fundamental human rights, meaningful to the majority section of our society. For example, the Indian constitution stipulates the right to practice religion and the right to conserve distinct language, culture and script. But, as we all know, there have been systematic attempts to undermine such secular and democratic foundations of the Indian polity. We need to deliberate if secessionist forces in Kashmir or North-East can be curtailed only through the repressive machinery of the state. Or, should we look for political solutions in Kashmir and the North-East so that the human rights are preserved for all groups in these areas. At the same time, we have to disapprove of the atrocities committed by the militants upon those sections of the civil society who refuse to toe their political line. We also have to support the functioning of the National Human Rights Commission and State Human Rights Commission. But a mere reliance upon these agencies will not ensure the enjoyment of human rights by the vast sections of the Indian society. What is required, as I see it, is generation of popular pressures from below to keep the State on its guard. After all, people are the best guardians of democracy. In this context, seminars as the present one are of crucial importance.

I would like to end this submission by referring to another unfortunate trend in international politics in the context of human rights. This relates to the issue of human rights being used by the US-led Western industrialised States to justify their continuing interventions in international politics. This trend has particularly increased with the dissolution of the Soviet bloc and the establishment of American unipolarism. For instance, we can cite the gross violation of human rights by the USA in Iraq, and of American bombing of alleged terrorist bases in Libya or Afghanistan. Washington can also be accused of adopting a double standard on human rights. While China is regularly condemned for the events of Tienanmen Square, the USA has been propping up dictatorial and conservative forces in Latin America, Africa and Asia. Again India is taken to task for violating the human rights in Kashmir, Punjab and North-East, but there is American silence both on Islamabad's violation of human rights within Pakistan as well as in the Pakistan Occupied Kashmir. I would argue that progressive and democratic forces have to stand up against the dichotomous American attitude of human rights, if we have to adopt a 'holistic' approach to the notion of human rights. We have to realise the crucial fact that guarantee for human rights in a bourgeois democratic State India will not be possible unless the popular struggle for human rights within the States become coterminous with the struggle against imperialism and colonialism. With these few words, I have a very great pleasure in inaugurating the seminar, which I am sure will be very fruitful and thought-provoking.

# The Rights of the Other: Some Questions

4

*Ishita Mukhopadhyay*

This question of women's rights are being widely discussed and inclusion of these rights within the broader agenda of human rights has been welcome by international community. Protection of rights of women along with other disadvantaged has become one of the most integral part of human rights. The paper revisits the question of rights of women and the approach of the premise of inclusion within human rights. It also tries go beyond the protective rights and analyses the socio-economic context of these rights. Section I deals with the question as represented in the literature of human rights. Section II goes beyond protective rights and presents the context of incidence of violence against women. Section III lists some other rights and legitimacy of inclusion of them in the question of human rights. Section IV puts the bottom line to the whole story.

## I

"Human rights and human development share a common vision and a common purpose—to secure the secure, well-being and dignity of all people everywhere. To secure:

- Freedom from discrimination—by gender, race, ethnicity, national origin or religion.
- Freedom from want—to enjoy a decent standard of living.
- Freedom from fear—of threats to personal security, from torture, arbitrary arrest and other violent acts.
- Freedom from injustice and violations from the rule of law.

- Freedom of thought and speech and to participate in decision-making and form associations.
- Freedom for decent work—without exploitation."

These are the words of introduction of Human Development Report, 2000. The focus of this report is the agenda of human rights. The inclusion of women's rights can be easily spotted in the agenda. It is included within protective rights against all discrimination. The report also acknowledges the fact that rising women's movement in the decade of the eighties and nineties has been successful in inclusion of gender within the construction of human rights. Much has been the contribution of the Convention on the Elimination of All Forms of Discrimination Against Women (CEDAW). It was also mentioned in the report that even apart from the issue of gender mentioned only under the broad heading of discrimination, all the other kinds of freedom have their spaces divided between the genders. We have a gendered vision of freedom in all these aspects. All the questions of freedom can be looked through the gender lens.

The report makes a mention of some of them. It was stated that the right to have freedom from fear is not protected as worldwide approximately 1.2 million women and girls under 18 are trafficked for prostitution each year and the issue of protection against inflicted violence against women requires public awareness. Again, it was mentioned that the right to have protection against injustice would mean termination of domestic violence and would be translated in revision of domestic laws.

The question of security has been dealt widely as the recorded largest personal threat has been experienced by women all over the world. Mention has been made of rape, trafficking and female genital mutilation. Attention has also been drawn towards higher incidence of domestic violence and 'honour killings'. It was presented that worldwide one in every three women on the average has been reported to be victim of violence in an intimate relationship. The question of dealing with HIV/AIDS was also adequately mentioned. This was the approach to the question of women's rights from the angle of human development.

The approach to some extent is an echo of what CEDAW tried to project. CEDAW was adopted in 1979 and Human Development Report, 2000 had incorporated CEDAW norms as the norms of human development. There is absolute international consensus in acknowledging CEDAW as one of the movers and shakers of the question of women's rights throughout the world.

It was recorded that women's rights are violated in three aspects:

- Discrimination in economic, political and social opportunities.
- Inequality in family life.
- Gender-based violence.

The ultimate way to achieve these rights is going towards women empowerment. Again if we observe the message, it was a comprehensive one. The coverage of women's rights was considered with respect to denial of socio-economic justice, but as these clauses were reread in 2000 in Human Development Report and elsewhere, the emphasis fell on the issue of gender based violence in many of the international ratifications.

The subordinate status of women was also reported in the World Conference of Human Rights in Vienna in 1993. Here it was stated that women's rights are "an inalienable, integral and indivisible part of universal human rights". Human Rights Watch Women's Rights Project, an independent project released its findings in 1998 on violation of women's rights. These included incidences of violence on women in the domestic and external sphere. Emphasis was again rested on violence and the right to have protection from gender-based violence.

Equality Now is the name of another organization which was founded in 1992 to work for the protection and promotion of the human rights of women around the world. In the 1998-99 Report of this organization sixteen areas of women's action have been listed where women's rights have been violated and worldwide action is required. The areas are listed below:

- Reproductive rights in Poland.
- Gender-based political asylum in Canada.

- Rape and genocide in Bosnia.
- Trafficking of women to Japan.
- Efforts to stop female genital mutilation.
- Rape in South Africa.
- Domestic violence and judicial bias in the United States.
- Medicalisation of female genital mutilation in Egypt.
- Gender-based political asylum in the United States.
- Abortion imprisonment in Nepal.
- Consideration of women in the election of United Nation's Secretary-General.
- Sex tourism from the United States.
- Censorship of the campaign against female genital mutilation in the Gambia.
- Slavery in Ghana.
- Imminent execution of battered women and her defenders in Trinidad and Tobago.
- Holding governments accountable in the Beijing + 5 Review process.

If we observe the above areas of action, the emphasis and significance seem to feature the different forms of gender-based violence and denial of protective rights.

We have reviewed some of the noted literature on the question of women's rights. Although a large amount remains still to be discussed, we can capture the main trends in international mindset. The dominance in thought regarding gender-based violence can be explained by the empirical data on increasing violence against women—both in the private and public sphere around the world. These prioritized protective rights against violence over all other forms of rights recognized, but yet to be emphasized in the discussions.

## II

Looking at the context of incidence of violence, there have been attempts at explanations both at the micro level and macro levied contexts as represented by Renzetti, Edleso, and Bergen

(2001). The micro-based explanations have been categorized as social learning theory, psychopathology, psychological and physiological explanations, resource theory and exchange theory. The macro-oriented theories focus on cultural acceptance of violence, patriarchy of feminist perspectives, sub-culture of violence, and structural stress. If we look at the micro-based theories they are all trying to explain why individuals perform violent acts upon women in particular. Hence, they try to relate violence to family, to socio-cultural context, and role of external agents like alcohol. These are not entirely isolated from the macro theories who try to explain more the attitude. While patriarchy governs, violence is seen as a means to subordinate the other sex.

However, it we go beyond explaining specific acts of violence upon women, violence against women takes certain forms throughout the world. There are incidences of domestic as well as external violence. Domestic violence is no doubt an expression of subordination, but the psychology of violence ends with the question as to why violence was used as a means. This is specifically so when violence leads to death of the victim. The gendered attitude of the society always tends to look at acts of violence inflicted on women as less offensive than a general act of violence. A woman is under subordination and hence can be subject to any kind of violent act. But this subordination starts from the gendered construction of the household and family. Much has been said and written over gendered composition of the household. As we recognize it, violence against women takes slightly different form than the general pattern of violence. Body and sexuality of the woman is mostly subject to violence. This pattern of violence cannot be explained except looking at its origin in the household.

The concept of marriage and the position of marriage in a women's life need to be looked into to get the answer. As paternity is something which none other than the mother of the child can tell, paternity was required to be defined. Maternity is naturally biologically defined. To define the paternity, there has to be a marriage contract and sexuality of the woman is to be controlled. Thus, the family became historically a weapon to control this body of the woman. Again, the essence of a well-defined fatherhood cannot be explained without bringing the context of private property. Since we know that the right to private property and the need to define the ownership of private property would need well-defined fatherhood, this automatically indicated control over the body of women. This also implied that the identity of the woman was to be explained in terms of the position and relationship of the woman with respect to the family. Relationship becomes the identity of the woman—as mothers, daughters and wives. Controlled sexuality and body has become the form of violence in many respects.

The origin of this controlled sexuality was experienced right from hunter-gatherer society as narrated long ago by Engle in 1884. In his words:

> The 'savage' warrior and hunter had been content to take second place in the house, after the woman; the 'gentler' shepherd, in the arrogance of his wealth, pushed himself forward into the first place and the woman down into the second. And she could not complain. The division of labour within the family had regulated the division of property between the man and the woman. That division of labour had remained the same; and yet it now turned the previous domestic relation upside down, simply because the division of labour outside the family had changed. The same cause which had ensured to the woman her previous supremacy in the house—that her activity was confined to domestic labour—this same cause now ensured the man's supremacy in the house: the domestic labour of the woman no longer counted beside the acquisition of the necessities of life by the man; the latter was everything, the former an unimportant extra. We can already see from this that to emancipate woman and make her the equal of the man is and remains an impossibility so long as the woman is shut out from social productive labour and restricted to private domestic labour. The emancipation of woman will only be possible when woman can take part in

> production on a large, social scale, and domestic work no longer claims anything but an insignificant amount of her time. And only now has that become possible through modern large-scale industry, which does not merely permit of the employment of female labour over a wide range, but positively by demands it, while it also tends towards ending private domestic labour by changing it more and more into a public industry.

This narration historically introduced the first conceptual divide between the private sphere and public sphere of the other gender. This also explained how the rush for ownership of private property was historically the source of subordination. Re-reading Engle's thought of 1884 in the twenty-first century, the controlled sexuality and body of woman can be easily explained. While we now encounter an intermingling of private and public sphere, the story of subordination, control over body and sexuality continues in the public sphere. Public sphere becomes an extended private sphere with housewife action of activities. Control, subordination ultimately takes the course of violence as a means. Though violence can be explained by patriarchy, but patriarchy has got alliance with the process of production and reproduction. Thus, private property, the need to identify paternity has led to violence in a gender form.

Due to the same reasons cited above, apart from specific acts of violence against women, any general act of violence like communal violence, border conflicts and the like take a gendered form. People belonging to one community tend to attack the females of the other community to attack the masculinity of the males of the other community. Thus, the specific acts of violence as well as the general ones have got their causes embedded in the socio-economic roots.

## III

The above discussion has led to the general conclusion that unless we can extend our discussion of women's rights to the broad socio-economic issues, unless we go beyond protective right, we cannot deal with the rights of women with its fullest coverage. The rights of women need to be seen in the context of gendered versions of human rights. Looking at only protective rights as women's rights would be a neck submission to the gendered representation of family that patriarchy represents. To go beyond patriarchy we have to look beyond the range of protective rights. In this section, we will be considering some of the other rights which should be considered with equal emphasis in the literature of rights. The importance of socio-economic context in the question of women's rights has been discussed at length in Human Development Report in South Asia (2000), but this is yet to get recognition from the broad international community.

The first of these other issues concentrates on land. Women specially in the context of South Asia are alienated from land. Land as well as other property are owned by the household. Not only agricultural land, but household land is owned by household and given the gendered composition of the household, this is owned by the male head of the household. We are not entering into the discussion on why women should have the right to land and property. The issue has been extensively discussed by Agarwal (1994). But right to land should be among the agendas in discussion of women's rights. The academic and activist forums gave attention to the question of deprivation of land and other property by household in general, but little has been written, said and researched on deprivation of land rights of women. This again implies a reinforcement of the fact of alienation of women from private property.

Close to the discussion of land rights, comes the legitimacy of the right to food security. The issue has been raised in the literature by Dreze and Sen (1995), (1999). Intra-family food differential has empirical basis also. Its origin is also the same structured family and subordination of women within the family. But again this is an issue which is yet to take its place in the general discussion of women's rights.

Looking closely at the composition of the family, reproductive rights are also to be considered. The broad spectrum of reproductive rights include the following:

- right to decide the age of marriage.
- right to decide over marriage.

- right to decide the number of children.
- right to decide the spacing of children.
- right to safe motherhood.
- right to a good reproductive health.

As can be easily inferred, the right to good reproductive health will be denied if the right to good health is generally denied to women. This has been discussed with the help of empirical evidence from some countries by Sen and Presser (2000). Women as a means of reproduction has also consequent in denial of some of the basic reproductive rights to women in general. Subordination of the women within the family can be and has been the basis of deprivation with respect to reproductive rights. This is particularly true for women in the Third World. But this is also among the issues which is to take place at par with protective rights.

The right to education and the right to livelihood are also to take a place in the broad discussion of women's rights. These are areas for empowerment of women, but over and above empowerment, denial of these benefits would be denial of basic rights to women in particular.

The issue of women's rights should be seen as an issue not alienated from the general discussion of the rights of deprived ones. This is so as all forms of deprivation are gendered in character. So besides the demand for the rights of the deprived, there should be equal space for the rights of women deprived. The trend of socio-economic forces tend to orient the context of women's rights to the protective rights only. However, one can easily see that protective rights can be restored, while denial of some basic rights can continue. The socio-economic cause of violence are embedded in denial of these rights. The right to property, to work, to health, to education, to food security are all required to eliminate violence against women. This is not to undermine the importance of protective rights, but this is only to reinforce the situation of protective rights. All these rights supplement each other. Silence with respect to anyone of them would mean a weakening of the voice of the others. Violence against women is hard to be eliminated through acts and legislation only, while denial of basic rights continue. We have also the evidence of increasing violence on women though there has been absolute international consensus on elimination of all sorts of violence against women.

The context of rights can be questioned thus if it is confined only to the protective rights. The questions raised in this paper only places the issue of women's rights to the broad context of human rights and treatment of deprivation in the society in general. Discussion on these issues and expansion of the area of rights can continue. The paper has not tried to give an exhaustive list of women's rights to be considered, but some pertinent questions have been raised in the context of the literature discussing the agenda of women's rights in general.

## REFERENCES

Agarwal, B. 1994. *A Field of One's Own: Gender and Land Rights in South Asia*, Cambridge: Cambridge University Press.

Ahuja, R. 1998. *Violence Against Women*, New Delhi: Rawat Publication.

A. Sen and Presser (ed.) 2000. *Women's Empowerment and Demographic Processes,* Oxford: Oxford University Press.

Dreze, J. and Sen, A. 1999. *India, Economic Development and Social Opportunity*, Oxford: Oxford University Press.

Dreze, J. and Sen, A. 1995. 'Introduction to the Political Economy of Hunger', *Political Economy of Hunger* (ed.) J. Dreze, A. Sen, and Hussain, Oxford: Clarendon Press.

Engels, F.A. (1884) [1972]. *The Origin of the Family, Private Property and The State*, Penguin Books.

Equality Now 1998-99, Women's Action Network. http://www.equalitynow.org/english/wan/ wan_en.html

Human Rights Watch. 1998. *Global Report on Women's Human Rights.* India: Oxford University Press.

Renzetti, Edleson, and Bergen (ed.) 2001. *Violence Against Women.* New Delhi: Sage Publications.

United Nations Development Programme, 2000. *Human Development Report, 2000.* Oxford: Oxford University Press.

United Nations Development Programme, 2000. *Human Development Report in South Asia, 2000,* Pakistan: Oxford University Press.

# Dalits and Human Rights

*Debi Chatterjee*

5

Dalits comprise the most marginalised section of India's population. Socio-cultural and economic factors have, for thousands of years, entrenched the marginalisation of the 'untouchable castes' that form the core of the Dalit population. Caste stratification, rooted in Hindu religion, made for the inhuman degradation of a section of the population stigmatizing them as polluting and hence untouchable, leading to their persistent exclusion from goods and services. The products of their labour, of course, were not ostracized. In fact, their stigmatization formed the basis of the surplus extraction of their labour. Marked out as an identity group on the basis of their caste, they were doomed to perform certain demeaning jobs which were essentially labour-intensive, physically hazardous, and of low remunerative value. Aspirations for wealth, power and status were cut at the roots in the name of god and the god-stipulated caste norms, as members of the low Sudra castes were prohibited by religious stipulations from accumulating the fruits of their labour. This Brahminical order of society developed from the later Vedic period and crystallized over time into a rigid stratification system. Time and again, ritual power and state authority joined hands to ensure the smooth continuance of the order.[1]

Needless to say, Dalits, who happen to be amongst the weakest sections of the population, have proved to be extremely vulnerable to the adverse impact of globalisation in view of their traditional exclusion from the socio-economic and power structures. It is feared that with increasing emphasis on privatization, the growing discrimination against the rural, agricultural and informal sectors, the socio-economic exclusion of the Dalits is all set to be reinforced. Shrinkage of the public sector has as its corollary the shrinkage of the reserved zone for the Dalits. Rolling back of the subsidies that have come alongside has meant added hardships for those who were, given the social odds, already at a disadvantage. They have been particularly hard hit in terms of employment, food security, health and education.[2]

Since the early 1990s, violence against the Dalits has been escalating dramatically against the backdrop of the economic reforms associated with liberalization and privatisation. All this despite the fact that the Indian Constitution assures to all citizens equality before the law and equal protection of the law, alongside a host of other fundamental rights.

## I

Now, post-90s, have thrown up the need for major re-thinking of strategies of struggles of the Dalits. Against the backdrop of globalisation, efforts are already being made by the Dalits to (a) bring in new issues into focus in the course of their struggles, (b) develop new tools and techniques of struggles to supplement the existing ones, and (c) to search out new support bases in combating their marginality.

The '90s saw several major developments in the field of Dalit assertion. One of the most important developments has been the formation of the National Campaign on Dalit Human Rights. The National Campaign on Dalit Human Rights (NCDHR) was officially launched in India in December 1998 to act as a non-political secular forum comprising of a band of Dalit scholars and activists. The purpose was to promote solidarity, cooperation, and collective action at the national level for the promotion of Dalit human rights. Its efforts were largely directed towards demonstrating the link between Dalit issues and human rights issues. The move came against the backdrop of worldwide activities centring around the completion of fifty years of the Universal Declaration of Human Rights.

When other human rights activists and institutions in India were planning to celebrate the completion of the fiftieth year of the promulgation of Universal Declaration of Human Rights

(UDHR) as a response to the call of the United Nations, seventy-eight Dalit activists and human rights activists from across the country, concerned about the frequent atrocities and the blatant lack of implementation of the SC/ST (Prevention of Atrocities) Act of 1989, met in Bangalore to discuss a Programme of Action, deliberated and resolved to make use of this opportunity to "highlight the issue of Caste and Untouchability" among the International Community, International Organisations including the UN bodies and especially in UNCHR.

This paved the way for the promotion of National Campaign on Dalit Human Rights (NCDHR), which gathered massive support from various Dalit activists, including Dalit intellectuals, academics, bureaucrats, NGOs, Dalit organisations/movements, Dalit trade unions, writers and journalists, etc. Thus, the inauguration of the campaign took place on 10 December 1998 with the submission of 50,000 signatures and the Campaign Memorandum to the President of India. This was followed by the drafting of an Inaugural Folder with a Charter of Dalit Human Rights.

The NCDHR brought together Dalit activists from different states and union territories in India and focused on raising awareness amongst Dalits, government institutions, civil society and the press that violation of Dalit rights are in fact violation of human rights. It launched signature campaigns, organised national public hearings, held press conferences, issued press releases and undertook the release of campaign literature. It also met dignitaries including the President, the Prime Minister of India, National Human Rights and Women's Commission Members to impress upon them the urgency of the matter. Its efforts were not confined within India. Outside the country's borders, the NCDHR stepped up efforts to mobilize opinion on the Dalit question. The NCDHR played an important role in mobilizing opinion on the Dalit question in relation to the Durban Conference on Racism (2001), at the Asian Social Forum meet at Hyderabad (2003), and at the World Social Forum at Bombay (2004).[3]

It may be noted that the campaign was not set up as an attempt to subsume, replace or negate ongoing efforts of Dalits and others in various mass movements, people's organizations, labour unions, etc. Rather, it is an effort to galvanize all these movements into a representative body that can collectively organize, educate, agitate and demand for an end to untouchability and casteism once and for all in both the government and civil society. The main objectives of the NCDHR are to:

- Create awareness and support for Dalit human rights by highlighting the issues of Dalit human rights in civil society.
- Strengthen the unity and solidarity of Dalits and Dalit movements across the nation and the world.
- Prepare status reports on Dalits covering the areas of livelihood, education, land and labor, gender equity for Dalit women, life and security, and reservation and employment.
- Pressurize Central and State governments and State and National level statutory bodies to give top priority to Dalit rights.
- Pressurize statutory bodies of the UN and other international organizations to give top priority to Dalit issues.
- Highlight the culture and contribution of Dalit communities to society.

The ultimate aims are to ensure:

- That India and the International Community recognize and uphold that Dalit rights are human rights and decide to abolish effectively untouchability.
- To cast out caste so as to build a new, just social order.[4]

## II

Another major landmark in the field of Dalit assertion came in December 2001 with the formation of a National Conference of Dalit Organisations (NACDOR) as a confederation of more than some three hundred grass root Dalit organisations from across India. NACDOR is the founder of World Dignity Forum and is closely linked with the World Social Forum, GCAP, MDG and other International Campaigns.[5]

In NACDOR I, which was organized between 8-10 December 2001, we saw the participation of about one hundred and fifty Dalit organisations from fifteen states. Since then, many other Dalit organisations approached and joined NACDOR. In less than five years, NACDOR emerged as a powerful assertion of the Dalits. NACDOR on the occasion of India Social Forum in New Delhi, ensured the participation of more than three hundred partner Dalit organisations.[6]

Shortly after NACDOR I, a conference of Dalit intellectuals and activists met at Bhopal in Madhya Pradesh on 12 and 13 January 2002, to deliberate on issues pertaining to the welfare and justice of the Dalit population and chart out a new course of action for Dalits for the 21st century. A Declaration was unanimously adopted at the conference incorporating a 21-Point Action Agenda. This came to be known as the Bhopal Declaration. It outlined the delegates' faith in Ambedkar's teachings as well as in the UN's human rights discourse, making special mention of the Universal Declaration of Human Rights. It highlighted, inter alia, the need to 'make reservation mandatory in the private and corporate sector in the same proportion as in the public sector...'. And 'develop the capacities and skills of Dalits to help them cope up with the demands of these different sectors'. It also emphasised the need for the Dalits to make common cause with other liberation and human rights movements in and outside the country.[7]

The process of organising NACDOR II, *Vision and Voices of New Dalit,* was launched on 13 November 2006 in New Delhi. Mr. Digvijay Singh, former Chief Minister of Madhya Pradesh, Mr. Sharad Yadav, former Minister in the Central Government and President of Janta Dal (U), Mr. Sanjay Paswan, former Central Minister, Mr. Ram Das Athavale, MP, Industrialist and founder of Amity University. Dr. Ashok K. Chauhan, Mr. Arjun Dangle renowned Dalit Writer, Professor Jean Dreze economist and co-worker of Professor Amartya Sen, Ms. Kiran Sharma, Programme Director of Poorest Areas Civil Society Programme participated in the deliberations.[8] In the

Golden Jubilee Year of Dhamma Chakka Parvartan Day by Baba Saheb, Mr. Ashok Bharti, Convener of NACDOR proposed Panchsheela for the overall empowerment of the Dalits, which were adopted by all by a voice vote.

The adopted principles are:

1. Struggle for Land and Natural Resources,
2. Education,
3. Health,
4. Employment and Entrepreneurship,
5. Dignity—Leadership, caste annihilation, justice, etc.[9]

## III

Beyond the borders of India, from the late 1990s, Dalit Solidarity Networks were set up in different countries to promote the cause of Dalit human rights. They brought under their folds individuals as well as concerned groups. Besides, they linked up with international human rights organisations like Amnesty International and Human Rights Watch for the purpose. Seminars and workshops were organised, websites put up, signature campaigns and petitioning were undertaken. NCDHR established contacts with members of the National Dalit Solidarity Networks functioning in different countries.

In March 2000, the International Dalit Solidarity Network (IDSN) was formed. It is a network of national solidarity networks, groups from affected countries and international bodies concerned about caste discrimination. It aims at linking grassroot priorities with international mechanisms and institutions to establish 'Dalit rights' as 'human rights'. Its work involves encouraging the UN, EU and other bodies to recognise the fact that caste-based discrimination must be treated as a central human rights concern. In relation to the UN, its lobbying is directed mainly at the Human Rights Commission, the Sub-Commission for Civil and Political Rights and the UN Committee on the Elimination of Racial Discrimination (CERD) among others.

From the 1990s onwards, the Dalit struggles thus moved to the international arena. For the first time, the caste question was discussed at the World Conference on Human Rights at Vienna in 1993. Thereafter, it was raised at the World Summit on Social Development held at Copenhagen in 1995. However, caste-based discrimination in other countries was generally little discussed at the international or national levels. For the first time, a detailed critical examination of the system by the UN took place in 1996. Thereafter, the debate continued in different treaty-based bodies.[10]

An important effort to bring the issue of violation of Dalit's human rights into the agenda of the UN was attempted in the context of the Durban Conference on Racism, 2001. The World Conference against Racism was held from 31 August to 7 September 2001 in Durban, South Africa. It was the Third World Conference on this issue. The previous world conferences had been held in 1978 and 1983 and had primarily focused on ending apartheid in South Africa.

At the Third World Conference in 2001, the Member-States of the UN focused on the causes and consequences of various manifestations of racism, strengthening existing human rights mechanisms and UN conventions (such as Convention on the Elimination of All Forms of Racial Discrimination), and developing practical, action-oriented measures and strategies to combat contemporary forms of racism and intolerance.

From the Dalit perspective, the WCAR was a rare opportunity to raise the visibility of India's "hidden apartheid" at the international level. It was a crucial opportunity for Dalit groups to come together on a common platform and make a united stand against caste discrimination before the international community and the UN. Through one voice, a common strategy, joint lobbying and advocacy, and the mutual support of other communities and organizations from across the globe, Dalits sought to influence the content of the final resolutions adopted by the Member-States so that they reflected Dalit realities. WCAR consisted of both an Inter-Governmental (IG) Conference and a parallel NGO Forum. In the former, the governments of the UN Member-States were the decision-makers, while the NGOs primarily participated as lobbyists, observers and information providers. Although NGOs did not have the right to vote at the

IG Conference, they had a variety of opportunities to influence the agenda, direction and outcome of the conference. At the conference, Dalit groups from across the world with support from several international human rights organisations fought a tough battle for the inclusion of caste in the official charter on race as a form of descent based discrimination. Unfortunately however, they lost the battle in face of the hostility of the Indian government, but they did succeed in making their point.[11]

The Dalit contingent of more than a hundred and sixty activists was one of the largest and best organized non-governmental delegations present, and drew strong international support from governments, UN officials, and India's own National Human Rights Commission.

On December 23, 2002, the United Nations Committee on the Elimination of Racial Discrimination in concluding its discussions on descent-based discrimination, strongly condemned caste practices as violative of the International Convention on Elimination of All Forms of Racial Discrimination. It noted that "fresh efforts, as well as intensification of existing efforts, need to be made at the level of domestic law and practice, in order to eliminate the scourge of descent-based discrimination and empower communities affected by it". Among the recommendations of the Committee on Elimination of Racial Discrimination are the following: (a) to resolutely implement legislation and other measures already in force; (b) to formulate and put into action a comprehensive national strategy with the participation of members of the affected communities, including special measures in accordance with articles 1 and 2 of the Convention, in order to eliminate discrimination against members of descent-based groups; (c) to educate the general public on the importance of affirmative action programmes designed to address the situation of victims of descent-based discrimination; (d) to ensure where relevant, that judicial decisions and official actions take the prohibition of descent-based discrimination fully into account; and (e) to take substantial and effective measures to eradicate poverty among descent-based communities, and combat their social exclusion or marginalisation.[12]

On April 19, 2005, the UN Commission on Human Rights decided to appoint two Special Rapporteurs to tackle the entrenched problem of caste-based discrimination. In doing so it was endorsing an earlier decision taken by its Sub-commission on the Promotion and Protection of Human Rights to conduct a comprehensive analysis of the problem and find solutions for its eradication. The Sub-commission is to now undertake a three-year study, led by the two 'Special Rapporteurs', and draft a set of Principles and Guidelines to eliminate this form of discrimination.

The decision of the Commission came in the wake of an International Consultation held in Kathmandu in 2004 on how to address the problem. The Consultation adopted what is known as the Kathmandu Dalit Declaration,[13] which provided concrete proposals not only for governments, the UN and development agencies, but also for the private sector, trade unions and international financial institutions. One of the proposals was fulfilled in the form of the appointment of the Special Rapporteurs.

## IV

In the wake of the overall activism surrounding the UN Durban Conference on Racism, a large number of civil rights organizations and NGOs in the West revealed active interest in the Dalit problem. These included, inter alia, Anti-Slavery International, Lutheran World Federation, Asian Human Rights Commission, India Committee of the Netherlands, Minority Rights Group, Christian Aid, Oxfam, Amnesty International, Human Rights Watch, Holdeen India Programme and Commonwealth Human Rights Initiative. A couple of examples given below will demonstrate the nature of concern as was widely expressed on the issue.

On March 21, 2001, marking the International Day for the Elimination of Racial Discrimination, Human Rights Watch called for an end to caste-based discrimination around the world. Human Rights Watch saw the forthcoming World Conference against Racism, Racial Discrimination, Xenophobia and Related Intolerance which was to take place in Durban from August 31 to September 7, 2001 as a significant opportunity for the international community to address the situation of South Asia's large Dalit population. The organization was extremely critical of the attitude of the Government of India and decried its attempts to sabotage the efforts of Indian NGOs to raise awareness of the caste struggle at the preparatory meetings in the lead-up to the conference.[14]

HRW in its recommendations at Durban noted, inter alia, that 'nationally, concerned governments must act to uphold their own constitutional principles and international treaty obligations and work towards the full enjoyment of rights by all citizens, regardless of caste or descent. Globally, the international community must take advantage of the opportunity this World Conference represents to make progress on one of the world's most severe and forgotten abuses'. It also stated specifically, 'All governments, and in particular those of countries whose citizens suffer from caste or descent-based discrimination and abuse, should ratify and fully implement the International Convention on the Elimination of All Forms of Racial Discrimination.'

These apart, Human Rights Watch opined that:

> All governments should support efforts to implement the resolution on discrimination based on work and descent adopted by the UN Sub-commission on the Promotion and Protection of Human Rights in August 2000;
>
> Concerned governments should extend invitations to the special rapporteur on racism to investigate caste-based discrimination and other forms of discrimination based on descent in their respective countries;
>
> All governments should ensure that caste-based and similar discrimination against marginalized populations is explicitly addressed in the declaration and programme of action of the WCAR, and any follow-up plan of action thereafter;
>
> Dalits in South Asia, Buraku people in Japan, and other populations in similar situations should be explicitly acknowledged as groups of people who have been subject

to perennial and persistent forms of discrimination and abuse on the basis of their descent.

Moreover, Human Rights Watch felt that, concerned governments should:

1. Establish a program and timetable to enforce the abolition of "untouchability", segregation, or similar practices.
2. Enact and fully enforce laws aimed at ending abuses associated with caste, such as child labour, bonded labour, land reform, manual collection of human waste, and forced prostitution or similar practices.
3. Monitor and publicize the extent to which existing laws to end caste discrimination have been implemented.
4. Allocate adequate funds for programs for the socio-economic and educational support of communities that have faced discrimination on the basis of caste or descent.
5. Ensure greater participation by the affected communities in civil administration, especially the administration of justice, including in key institutions such as the police and judiciary.
6. Ensure that all necessary constitutional, legislative, and administrative measures, including appropriate forms of affirmative action, are in place to prohibit and redress discrimination on the basis of caste, and that such measures—including those already instituted in Japan and India—are continued until discrimination is eliminated.
7. Launch nationwide public awareness campaigns regarding legal prohibitions on discrimination on the basis of caste or descent. This campaign should explain in simple terms what actions are legally prohibited and what recourse is available to victims of discrimination and abuse.
8. Provide political and financial support for programs of the United Nations and regional bodies to assist countries seeking to eradicate caste discrimination.

9· United Nations development agencies should pay particular attention to caste violence and caste discrimination, assess the impact of their existing programs with regard to caste, and develop programs and strategies designed to curb abuse and encourage accountability.[15]

The Asian Human Rights Commission, too, was no less sympathetic to the Dalit cause at Durban. Adopting an extremely critical stand on of the Indian Government's role, in a Statement issued in the wake of the developments at Durban, the Asian Human Rights Commission observed:

> The World Conference against Racism, Racial Discrimination, Xenophobia and Related Intolerance (WCAR), held in Durban, South Africa, from Aug. 31 to Sept. 7, 2001, has brought into sharp focus several extreme forms of discrimination. Among these is the issue of caste—more specifically, the issue of the Dalits—for caste became a highly visible issue during the international debate on racial discrimination. It became obvious during the conference that Indian diplomats, in their extreme activism to keep caste out of the final declaration of this world gathering and its work programme, not only brought the Indian government into high disrepute, but also brought down the moral standing of India before the eyes of the world. India also lost any possibility of claiming to be a world leader in the promotion and protection of human rights until it changes its public position on the caste issue. The international conscience, which is being awakened to one of the cruelest forms of discrimination after many centuries of neglect, is naturally questioning the Indian stand and is asking "What kind of nation is this?"[16]

Till the 1990s, Dalits living outside India had shown little interest in matters relating to the struggles being waged by Dalits in India. But, from the 1990s, the picture began to change. We find that the Dalit diaspora started showing an active interest in the plight of the Dalits in India to the extent that they successfully organized several conferences in different parts of the world to press for the protection of the human rights of Dalits in India and abroad. The first such conference was held at Kuala Lumpur, Malaysia in 1998, to be followed by a conference in London in 2000 and in Vancouver in 2003.[17]

## V

Today, Dalit marginalisation is sought to be addressed from more diverse angles than it was previously done. Much of this diversification is in the context of the altered realities of the globalising world. For example, one of the important issue areas to come into prominence is the private sector where marginalisation was already extensive. With the expansion of the private sector, the woes of the Dalits are likely to increase manifold, hence to provide them with a legitimate entry point into the private sector, the demand for 'private sector reservation' is rightly being raised.

Despite the new trends in mobilization in the wake of the changing scenario, the Dalit movement has till now remained essentially fragmented with major differences around questions of targets, leadership, coordination, 'graded inequality', lack of awareness and understanding of the complexities of the issues, widespread illiteracy, the rural-urban divide, political fragmentation, differences along religious lines and on attitudes towards religion, class differences and lack of coordination of movements across regions are some of the visible hurdles. Even as significant advances are noticeable in the field of global networking for Dalit human rights, effective networking amongst Dalit groups has hardly developed at the grassroot levels within the country. At the grassroot levels, Dalit struggles are still waged largely along earlier lines focussing on questions of reservations, education, land rights, displacement, and citizenship rights (where relevant, as in West Bengal). What appears to be in focus at such a level is a fragmented rights approach rather than a holistic human rights perspective. This is, by and large, the general observable pattern so far as the functioning of the Dalit political parties, pressure lobbies—SC/ST cells in government offices, Ambedkarites movements are concerned. To go beyond such styles of functioning and emphasise a holistic, integrated human rights perspective in handling the Dalit question remains the urgent need of the hour. The global attention which has already been generated will no doubt go a long way in helping to forge the links between people, organisations and issues in this context. However, caution in identifying friends and enemies would remain crucial.

## NOTES

1. Wendy Doniger and Brian K. Smith tr., *The Laws of Manu*, Penguin, New Delhi, 1991.
2. Vivek Kumar, 'Social Exclusion', *Magnifying Mal-Development: Alternative Economic Survey*, India, Rainbow Publishers, New Delhi, 2004, p. 151.
3. www.ncdhr.org
4. *Ibid.*
5. http://groups.google.com/group/wnta/msg/862f7216f416638b
6. www.nacdor.org/TEXT FILES/ what we do. htm
7. www.pucl.org/Topics/Dalit_tribal/2002/bhopal.htm
8. *Ibid.*
9. Indian organisations launch NACDOR II, 2006/11/21, http://editor.ekduniya.in/Action/news/gcapnews.2007-04-19.6155636170
10. Ambrose Pinto, "Caste Discrimination and U.N.", *Economic and Political Weekly*, 28 September 2002, p. 3989.
11. http://www.Dalits.org/WCAR.htm
12. Ambrose Pinto, *op. cit.*
13. www.nepalDalitinfo.20m.com
14. http://www.hrw.org/reports/2001/globalcaste/
15. *Ibid.*
16. http://www.ahrchk.net/statements/mainfile.php/2001statement/29/
17. For a detailed discussion of the conferences Debi Chatterjee, "Dalit Situation in India Since the 1990s: An Examination of Certain Issues and Trends", *Socialist Perspective*, Vol. 33, Nos. 1-2, June-September 2005.

# Civil Rights in India: Towards Framing a Contemporary History

6

*Siddhartha Guha Ray*

Eric Hobsbawm, the eminent historian of our times, observes, "India, of course, remains...by far the most impressive example of a Third World state that has...maintained unbroken civilian supremacy though whether this justifies the label 'the world's greatest democracy' depends on how precisely we define Lincoln's 'government of the people, for the people, by the people'." This remark certainly contains some elements of truth. No doubt, India could maintain an apparently uninterrupted civil governance among the Third World countries, and only for this reason our rulers often boast of elevating India in the position of 'the world's largest democracy'. At the same time Hobsbawm raised a very pertinent question, whether this feature alone can justify India's claim to be the 'largest and the greatest democracy' of the world? The present essay aims at answering this particular question whether the maintenance of civil governance could ensure a genuine democratic rule in India. In this context, the nature of the Indian Constitution, different laws enacted by our legislators, economic policies of the government and the accountability of the government in protecting the democratic rights and civil liberties of the Indian citizens would come within the realm of our discussion. All these aspects would definitely reveal the real faces of Indian democracy and at the same time show that, to what extent, the rights of the citizens are preserved in this 'largest democracy' of the world.

The Indian Constitution gave certain fundamental rights to the citizens. Rights to equality before law, rights regarding the freedom of speech, right to assemble or form any association or union, right to free movement in any part of India, right against exploitation, right to freedom of religion, right to life—all such important rights have been inserted in the Constitution as the fundamental rights. The Article 32 clearly states—if a citizen feels that any of his fundamental rights has been curbed, he has the right to move the Apex Court for seeking 'judicial remedy' but at the same time this Constitution says that the state can violate all such fundamental rights in the interests of its own 'security'. The Constitution has conferred immense powers upon the rulers to enact draconian acts and laws in flagrant violation of democratic norms and principles, subverting the fundamental rights of the citizens. Thus, the matter of Constitutional right in India has been turned into a hoax. Since our independence our rulers had enforced several Black Acts, curtailing the rights of the people.

The Constituent Assembly enacted the Preventive Detention Act (PD Act) in 1950. Sardar Ballabhbhai Patel, then the Union Home Minister, raised the bill. In time of introducing the bill in the floor of the Constituent Assembly, Patel told before the House that he had to spend "two sleepless nights" before introducing the bill. But considering the question of "security of the state", he took initiative to promulgate the law. It was stated in the law that the ruler could arrest or detain any person without trial for an indefinite period by enforcing this act. The PD Act empowered the rulers to detain any person suspected of hampering 'the security of the state', disturbing the 'maintenance of public order', or disrupting the 'maintenance of supplies and services essential to the community'. The first two points were meant for suppressing political dissent and the third one could be used for curbing trade union rights. Immediately after the Transfer of Power in 1947, the Communist Party of India resorted to armed insurrection. To add to it, militant upsurge of the poor peasants of Telengana broke out. The situation prompted the rulers to implement this act for suppressing the revolutionary activities of the people.

The Preventive Detention was enforced for a considerable length of time during the last fifty years in our country, in different names. During the Sino-Indian border conflict in 1962, a section of the Communist Party of India felt that it was not China but India was the aggressor state. They also questioned the legitimacy of the McMohan line determined by British imperialists. The Nehru Government at the Centre was prompted to suppress these 'anti-national' elements. The Parliament enacted the Defence of India Rules (DIR). This Act lacked any essential difference with the PD Act. Thousands of political workers were arrested and kept in jail without trial.

In 1971 elections, the ruling Congress of Indira Gandhi returned to power with a massive two-third majority. Within few weeks of her return to power, Mrs. Gandhi passed and imposed Maintenance of Internal Security Act (MISA), designed to suppress any kind of political dissent, particularly the Naxalite activities. This Act also empowered the rulers to detain any suspect hostile to the maintenance of internal security of the country. The intentions of the rulers were crystal clear. Any political movement or ideology that would expose the oppressive nature and endanger the existence of the rulers would be ruthlessly suppressed using this 'Black Act'.

By the mid-1970s, people throughout India protested against the authoritarian rule of Indira Gandhi. Mrs. Gandhi, in order to silent the voice of protest, declared internal emergency in India on June 26, 1975, in compliance with the provisions laid down in our Constitution. During the emergency many political organizations were banned, the right to form associations was curbed, freedom of press was suppressed and innumerable protagonists of hostile political view were kept under detention without trial. All the fundamental rights, proclaimed in the Constitution, were denied. The Amnesty International, in its annual report of 1977, observed—"The MISA and the DIR in particular, have been used extensively to detain peaceful opponents of the government, after the declaration of National State of Emergency on 26th June 1975." The same report stated, quoting the government statistics that during the Emergency 34,630 people were arrested under the MISA. The Emergency provision of the MISA, Article 16A, "permitted political detainee to be held without even being informed of the grounds of arrest". Added to it, thousands of citizens were held under DIR during the Emergency.

The ignominious defeat of the Congress in 1977 parliamentary polls put an end to the emergency. The Janata ministry was formed under the Prime Ministership of Morarji Desai in March 1977. On the eve of the election, the Janata Party in its election manifesto declared that the anti-people laws like MISA and PD Act were a "betrayal of the testament of the faith that the founding fathers bequeathed to the people" and such "laws were the culmination of a conspiracy to devalue democracy". But in power, their attitude changed. In December 1977, Home Minister Charan Singh introduced the Code of Criminal Procedure (Amendment) Act, 1977, incorporating Preventive Detention in the Criminal Procedure Code of the country and making the same an 'ordinary' law of the land. Prime Minister Morarji Desai told the Chief Ministers in November 1978, that Preventive Detention Acts were essential to maintain law and order in the states and advised them to promulgate such legislation in their respective states.

In 1985, when Rajiv Gandhi was the Prime Minister, the Parliament passed the infamous Terrorist and Disruptive Activities Act, 1985 (TADA). For ten years following 1985, the TADA was extensively used not only for suppressing the nationality struggles of the Punjab, Kashmir and North Eastern regions, but also against the minority community.

The TADA had a striking similarity with the Rowlatt Act, promulgated by the British rulers in 1919. On March 28, 1919, a week after the Viceroy gave his consent to the Rowlatt Act, Muhammad Ali Jinnah resigned from the Imperial Legislative Council and wrote to the Viceroy, "A government that passes or sanctions such a law in times of peace forfeits its claim to be called a civilized government." But never such a democratic voice of protest could be heard from any Indian legislator in the Parliament in time of enactment of the TADA. What seemed to be more unfortunate that the Supreme Court also in its judgement upheld this repressive Act. The British Rulers would generally brand the fighters for Indian freedom as 'terrorists'. The rulers of free India, stepping into shoes of their British masters, also did not hesitate to describe their political opponents as 'terrorists'. By applying the TADA, any person suspected of posing a 'threat to the public order' and challenging the 'very existence of sovereignty as well as the security of India' could be remanded into the custody for a period even extending up to two years. Like the Rowlatt Act, the TADA also had, within its framework, the provisions of appointing designated courts. The designated courts under TADA could try the victims not in a public place but in absolute concealment, even within the four walls of the jails. As for bail, the onus lay on the accused to give 'reasonable grounds for believing that' he was not guilty. The designated courts, framed under the TADA rule could even pronounce death sentence to the accused. The TADA was, however, withdrawn in 1995, thanks to tremendous public pressure.

Mention may be made of one more 'Black Act' which tends to violate the right to life of Indian citizens, in several places of the country. This is the Armed Forces (Special Power) Act (AFSPA). This Act gives unrestricted and absolute power to the army or paramilitary forces for suppressing the disturbing citizens. In fact, indiscriminate application of Armed Forces Special Power Act has turned many places of India into a battlefield. The Indian army, along with the paramilitary forces, have been engaged for waging a ruthless brutal war against the civil population in areas like Kashmir, North East Indian Provinces, etc. In 1958, the Union Home Minister G.B. Pant piloted the Armed Forces Special Power Bill in the Lok Sabha with the objective of conferring upon the armed forces the powers to arrest, interrogate, confine and even shoot to kill any person in such areas which will be declared 'disturbed' by notification issued by competent authority. The AFSPA was passed in the Parliament for suppressing the revolt of the Nagas without much debate or discussion. The Act empowered the army personnel to "arrest without warrant, any person, who has committed a cognizable offence or against whom a reasonable suspicion exists that he has committed or about to commit a cognizable offence and...enter and search without warrant any premises to make any such arrest." Under this Act "force can be used to the point of causing death on any person carrying any weapon or things capable of being used as a weapon or contravening an order prohibiting an assembly of five or more persons." In other words, the AFSPA gives the army an absolute power to commit massacre, rape, destruction of property and everything violating the rights of the people. But there exists virtually no provision for bringing the guilty army personnel under judicial scrutiny, as the Act says, "no prosecution, suit or other proceedings should be instituted, except with the previous sanction of the Central Government, against any person in respect of anything done or purported to be done in exercise of the power conferred by the Act." Experiences in Jammu and Kashmir and North Eastern provinces have clearly shown that the "sanction of the central government" for prosecuting the guilty army officers is very rarely achieved. The People's Union for Democratic Rights (PUDR) and the Naga People's Movement for Human Rights (NPMHR) challenged the constitutional validity of the AFSPA in the Supreme Court. But the writ had been pending before the Apex Court since 1982 and no hearing did take place till recently. Delhi High Court, however, found the Act constitutional on the ground that "a social purpose is fulfilled by the statute". Hence, the Parliament was justified in enacting the Act and its action, in this regard, was "just, fair and reasonable".

The rulers of 'independent India' absolutely depended, from the very beginning, on armed might for protecting their authority and for containing social discontent. They did not attribute much importance to the point of winning popular consent. The undemocratic rule and state terror in the last fifty years failed to give the Indians the dignity of free citizens. Our rulers deliberately ignored the socio-economic factors responsible for the protest movements and tried to project them as mere manifestations of law and order problems. The occasion of the Transfer of Power heard of a pledge by the Indian rulers that they would stand for the achievement of a society which "would ensure individual liberty, equality of opportunity and the fullest scope for every citizen for the development of his personality". The rulers on whom the powers were transferred on August 15, 1947, forgot that a popular consent formed the very basis of a free republic, in real sense of the term, and people's right to protest against injustice, oppression, exploitation and corruption is very much enshrined within the democratic principle of popular consent.

# Environment and Human Rights

7

*A.K. Ghosh*

## Introduction

Economic development in the present day world shifted with a new approach as modern technology evolved since the days of Industrial Revolution in Europe. Capital, labour and technology led to an expanding market cutting across continents; the soaring profit line was good enough incentive to invest more, produce more and market more products. Need-based life style changed into an era of consumerism. "Sky is the limit" concept gained ground till the decade of 1970s. Retrospection was deemed essential by a group of intellectuals; a study supported by 'Club of Rome' was published as a futuristic projection called "Limits to Growth" (Meadows et al., 1972). The 'World Model' includes equations in which the 'population growth increases with food output and in which the rates of resource depletion and pollution levels rise with the level of industrial output'. The time frame used was 1900 to 2100. It was observed that over the early path of the period, population and industrial output per capita continued to grow but model predicts that industrial output and food per capita will plunge and at the end the standard of living is likely to sink below the level prevailing in 1900.

This was indeed a 'Doomsday' scenario. One has to remember that the American author Racheal Carson predicted a 'Silent Spring' about five years before the publication of 'Limits to Growth'. These studies had stirred the Western world. Right to Environment seems to have grown out of consciousness of human society with the observance of the 'Earth Day' in April, 1970. A new beginning was made. A re-look at the very process if developmental economics, environmental policy and quality of life, were imperative (Baumol and Bates, 1979).

The lesson learned become clearer with increasing awareness about the inherent problem the path of development is likely to face. While population explosion in the developing world was blamed for all the ills, the trend of consumerism in the Western world was equally criticized in view of the fast resource depletion to meet the privileged 25 per cent at the cost of suffering 75 per cent.

The "World Conservation Strategy" (1980) called for a paradigm shift in the methods of development. Sustainable Development becomes the key word with enormous support from the report of the Bruntlund Commission.

### Lesson from 20th Century

The enormous development of science and technology empowered the human society to achieve new dimensions of economic prosperity. The advent of space science, remote sensing, nuclear power and finally the magic of microchips made the planet earth a wonderland. In the process, the finite resources started depleting at the fastest pace—the entire biosphere became arena for this new "mantra" of development. Land, water, atmosphere, forest and vegetation, freshwater and marine resource—each started pathological syndrome of degradation and suffered from man-made pollution load.

In May 1984, the World Resources Institute organized a meet of 75 experts from 20 countries to look at global resource and population problem and opportunities. The experts analyzed the situation and proposed initiatives for private and public action 'allaying the restive pessimism that stands between the world we have and the one we want' (Speth, 1985). The key word that emerged is again 'Sustainable Development'. The Global Possible Conference declared that several critical transitions that must be implemented. These include:

- A demographic transition to a stable world population of low birth and death rate.

- An energy transition to high efficiency in production and increasing reliance on renewable energy.
- A resource transition to reliance on nature's 'income' without depletion of its 'capital'.
- An economic transition to sustainable development and on broader sharing of its benefits.
- A political transition to a global negotiation keeping in tune the North and South, East and West.

It was suggested that such a prosperous and sustainable future is attainable.

## Trend of Globalization

However, while the global consensus on the sustainable development might have emerged by end of 1990s, the drive towards more freedom of trade and breaking down barriers for facilitating 'global market' economy, was seen only when the world accepted WTO prescription. To severe monopoly interest, the system of "Trade Related Intellectual Property Rights" (TRIPS) became a buzz word. Structural readjustment and free trade witnessed a changing scenario in international economy.

The Gross Domestic Product (GDP) in the World's fastest growing economies of China and India soared. In a boom time for generating more capital gain, the number of poor didn't decline. 'Agenda 21' adopted at the UN Conference on Environment and Development (UNCED), remained an unfulfilled pledge. The chasm between rich and the poor widened.

During this process, the state monopoly over natural resource at first became much stronger but with globalization, the so-called corporate efficiency in managing natural resources gained ground. Groundwater is being openly depleted by the MNCs at the cost of village water supply to manufacture "soft drinks" and "bottled water". Poor and marginalized lost their homestead land and agricultural land however small the holding may be, in the name of creating Special Economic Zone or in other developmental projects. Since Independence, at least 30 million rural Indians were evicted for only "Multipurpose River Valley

Projects". Millions lost land to other development project currently being pursued by private capital with state's support.

## Constitutional Rights: Policy

Indian Constitution has guaranteed "right to life" and "right to clean environment" but also underlined the duties of the citizens in exercising such rights. It's not only a part of fundamental rights guaranteed under Constitution of the Republic, it's also the policy of elected governments in a democracy surviving over last six decades since Independence.

The policy statements on environment however came much late in 1992 following action in setting up autonomous Pollution Control Boards at Central and the state level, way back in 1974. The environmental acts and rules promulgated since 1970s promise a clean and safe environment and lead one to dream a better quality of life. Acts and rules also led to setting up standards. Incentives for clean environment and disincentives for violation of laws were clearly publicized. But in reality, offenders often managed to go scot-free. Implementation of excellent set of legal instruments remained tardy. Citizens in India continued to suffer the deprivation from clean environment.

The failure of administrative bureaucracy perhaps sensitized the civil society. Environment Movement became the new events of Indian scenario. References to such movements can be found in several publications (Krishna, 1996; Dembowski, 2001).

The issue of human rights over environmental resource was first widely felt during "Chipko Movement" in Garhwal Himalayas in 1970s. The women's right to collect firewood from forests was denied leading to a non-violent movement; hugging the tree to prevent clear felling by contractors, saved not only forests but established women's rights to collect dried woods, lops and tops as only source of fuel. The Government of India enacted Forest (Conservation) Act in 1980 recognizing need for re-looking at forest's role in ecosystem functioning. The women's group also is related to have organized the largest voluntary afforestation programme through eco-development camps (Ghosh, 1989). While affected people established their rights over natural resources, elsewhere the citizens at large voiced their concern about possible negative impacts on one of the richest rain forest in Kerala due to a proposed Hydel Power Project. The years of 1980-83 witnessed "Save Silent Valley" movement; the movement forced the Central Government to review the project and accept people's verdict. 1980s also witnessed the now famous movement to prevent ecological disaster in the Doon Valley against limestone mining. Judicial verdict in 1985 finally enclosed 27 mining operation and led to reclamation of degraded land and afforestations. Such movements to establish people's rights can be chronicled from Koel-karo project area in Bihar through Balco project in Orissa to the most famous movement named 'Narmada Bachao Andolan', cutting across Madhya Pradesh, Maharashtra and Gujarat. While national media became increasingly sensitized over such mass based movements, state level case studies also demanded serious attention.

One such being the public interest litigation filed against conversion of 800 hectares of wetlands in east Calcutta. A movement organized by civil society and led by PUBLIC—a new born NGO, created media sensation and public interest; the verdict of the Calcutta High Court clearly went in favour of citizen's demand. Strangely, the same state government has now declared it as a "Ramsar Site"—Wetlands of international importance.

## Changing Policy: Participatory Management

The growing concern for environment gradually made inroads towards new policy formulation. The State and the Central Government felt the urge for decentralized system of governance and need for people's participation in conservation of natural resources.

The formation of Forest Protection Committee (FPC) under Joint Forest Management (JFM) policy of 1988 and similar opportunities extended for participation in Watershed Management or Minor Irrigation Management, bear testimony to people's power. The legal sanction for a compulsory public hearing during Environmental Impact Study, further established people's power. The government has at last published a

'Rehabilitation and Resettlement' Policy in 2005, a new 'Water Policy' advocated for a policy change towards 'Rainwater Harvesting'.

The 73rd and 74th Constitutional amendments empowered the local communities to establish a system of local self-governance including management of the vital natural resources like land and water. The Panchayati Raj system advocated implementation of such a process of decentralization. The environment movement in India led the judiciary to establish special "Green Branches" in the High Courts of Kolkata and Chennai. The Supreme Court of India also forced the government to take *suo motu* actions, one such being cleaning up Delhi's automobile pollution through changeover to CNG from conventional fuel. It is again, at the behest of a PIL, the Supreme Court forced the West Bengal Government to reallocate 400 odd tannery units in Kolkata with provision for a common effluent treatment plant and thereby minimize the chromium pollution of surface water.

The awareness in the civil society backed up by media had enforced a positive change of attitude in the system of governance. That felling of trees and conversation of wetlands are anti-environment, just to cite two examples, have now become a matter of common concern.

The civil society apart, the role of judiciary helped to establish human rights over environment. Collectively, the actions perhaps made the system of governance more alert and accountable.

The human society especially in the tropics depends heavily on biodiversity and biomass. Wild and domesticated biological resources provide all the food, fodder, a large percentage of rural fuel supply, building material, textiles, paper and pulp, medicinal and hundreds of other essentials, raw or value added such resources are now valued in billions of U.S. dollars. The Biological Diversity Act, 2002 and Rules, 2004, rightfully acknowledge the rights of the local community by suggesting Biodiversity Committee (BMC) at the local level; Preparation of "Peoples' Biodiversity Registers" (PBR) as a mandatory process of managing local resource is a vindication of human rights over local living resource.

To sum up, human society, now considered being composed of Biosphere People and Ecosystem People—the former outside the purview of specific ecosystem and the latter intimately linked with system—have been able to establish human rights over environment. Considering, environmental awareness, even globally, has a history of only four decades, establishing human rights over environment can be perceived as one of the fastest phenomenon in the modern times.

## REFERENCES

Baumol, William J. and Oates, Wallace, E. 1979. *Economics, Environmental Policy and the Quality of Life*. Prentice Hall Inc., N.J.

Dembowski, Hans 2001. *Taking the State to Court: Public Interest Litigation and Public Sphere in Metropolitan in India*. Oxford University Press, New Delhi.

Ghosh, Ashish 1989. Environmental Movements—A Brief Review. *Sci Tech Focus* (3&4): 30-32.

Krishna, Sumi 1996. *Environmental Politics: Peoples' Lives and Developmental Choices*. Sage Publications, New Delhi, London.

Meadows, Donella et al. 1972. *The Limits to Growth: A Report of the Club of Romes*. Project on the Predicament of Mankind. A Potomac Associates Book, published by Universe Books.

Repetto, Robert (ed). 1985. The Global Possible: Resources, Development and the New Century. Affiliated East West Press Pvt. Ltd.

# Refugees and Human Rights: Towards Refugee Protection Regime

8

*Sumita Sen*

## Introduction

In the post-Cold War years, the states are faced with new challenges of violent civil strives, terrorism, cross-border migration, upsurge of ethno-nationalism, human rights protection, economic growth inviting significant discourses on human security and human development. At the same time the years in between, have failed to rectify the global imbalances, that on many occasions were the cause of dissension and strife across the latitude. A striking feature of the world population is the co-existence of a few number of billionaires against more than a billion people living on less than US $1 a day. The continued increase in the number of refugees and the internally displaced persons alongside the other groups of unemployed, landless, poor and malnourished and illiterates are reflections of a disorder which development has failed to address the world over. The existing arrangements though guided by internationally accepted principles and norms are still lacking in guaranteeing adequate human rights protection to those deprived people in general. It is thus, no unforeseen circumstances or a chance that has brought in confusion in programmes at the international, national, regional and local levels which are set for people viz. citizens, refugees, internally displaced people (IDPs), stateless, illegal migrants, etc. Given the ongoing globalisation programmes and the movement for democracy and human rights guarantees, it becomes imperative to look for the reasons for failure on the part of the states and international bodies in addressing the problem of what UNHCR terms as 'people of concern'.

## The Refugee Scenario

The end of World War II and the end of Cold War brought in large scale population movement accompanied by decolonisation process within the regions. The cross border forced movement of masses, giving rise to the need for treating this phenomenon globally, was from Europe (east) to Europe (west), from Third World (south) to Europe and America (north), to Third World to mostly adjacent Third World countries. Currently, there are an estimated 2,07,51,900 refugees in the world comprising generally 8603600 in Asia, 51,69,300 in Africa, 2,51,300 in Latin America, 7,16,800 in North America and 36,66,700 in Europe, etc. In fact refugee records indicate that Asia accommodates almost 54% of all refugees followed by Africa of 30%, Europe 19% and North America 5%. The number indicates the complex nature of refugee issue under the socio-political and economic conditions alongside the weak protection institutions prevailing in the regions due to ethnic and civil conflicts, gross violations of human rights, pressure of economic development, weakening of state's role in the protection of the vulnerable groups, etc.

The increased number of political and ethnic conflicts alongside the common socio-cultural, ethnic roots in South Asian region made the region witness influx of unregistered immigrants, stateless and refugees. On the frontiers of inter-state relations the gradual increase of hostilities, mistrust and suspicion among the South Asian states have increasingly created refugee situations in the region. Some of the refugee conditions in South Asia are briefly presented below. The analysis of the cases of refugees and the unregistered immigrant population within the region will highlight the conditions of refugees and the policies adopted by the respective states for the population who ultimately flee their homes and cross borders.

The World Refugee Survey, 2003 mentioned that India alone hosts approximately 3,32,300 refugees and is one of the largest *refugee receiving* countries in South Asia.

(a) The developments following independence, i.e. the partition period followed by destruction and bloodshed saw millions of people belonging to different religions fleeing their home. An estimated 15 million people had to migrate from their homes. These people though were granted citizenship by both India and Pakistan.

(b) The Bangladesh war of independence made millions of Bangladeshis take shelter in India. While many of them have been provided citizenship, the conditions of the refugees did not indicate absolute protection under human rights regime. The reason though could be understood by the prevailing economic and political as well as strategic conditions in India.

(c) Following the crisis in Tibet, many Tibetans sought refuge in India and Nepal. While the Tibetans are accorded refugee status and are mostly accommodated in the Dharamsala, the nationality and citizenship of the Tibetans in India continue to haunt these refugees. On the other hand, the Nepal government forcibly sent many of the unwilling Tibetan refugees back to China. Nepal government's policy of repatriation of the Tibetans was seen as a gross violation of human rights of these refugees.

(d) Jumma refugees faced with severe atrocities from the Chittagong Hill Tracts constitute another large group of those who fled to India after the violent activities conducted by the Bangladesh security personnel. While many were provided shelter in Tripura as refugees, they were not satisfied by the basic amenities provided during their shelter years. On the other hand, the Accord between Bangladesh and India on repatriation and rehabilitation of these refugees to Bangladesh was not appreciated by those for whom it was reached claiming that many human rights and refugee rights were violated.

(e) The civil strife between the Sinhala and Tamil population in Sri Lanka is known for its long span of continuity. The fight for a separate homeland by the Tamils also led many to take refuge in India. While Sri Lankan refugees in India live in the refugee camps, many of them live outside the camps. One may find that these refugees have not been provided with all the basic human rights conditions.

(f) The Chin Burmese refugee crisis intensified with the military junta taking over the government control and mass violations of human rights making as many as 40,000 of them taking shelter in India. The problem with these people became complex as they are stateless on the one hand and are identified as illegal migrants in India making them deprived of any assistance to be sought as asylum seeker. It is often assumed that they are mostly victims of shifting political and foreign policy interests of India and are subject of forced deportation.

(g) The ethnic tension in Bhutan aggravated with the adoption of several laws relating to citizenship, religion, language, marriage, etc. The southern Bhutanese of Nepali origin began to flee their homes to neighbouring India and Nepal. While India did not grant them refugee status, most of them reached Nepal and are accommodated in several refugee camps set up by UNHCR in Nepal. While the conditions inside the camps were not deplorable but there are instances of violent resentment among the poor local population against these people. Several human rights bodies are demanding resolution of this problem of resettlement options. A recent report indicates that some of the refugees will be repatriated and rehabilitated in the US while the remaining will await the final solution of their problem.

The South Asian region while hosting a huge number of refugees, migrants stateless and the internally displaced peoples has no concrete set of refugee rights and duties. While this situation is often used in denying human rights protection to them, these groups are often considered as security threat. It is also known to many that geo-political considerations have taken priority over protection of refugees. On the other hand, often led these people are considered 'useful' for political leverage within the host countries for their interest in tacitly interfering in the domestic affairs of others more smoothly through them. Many a times these groups are made to be buffer population in the bordering areas. More often this category of population are subject to economic exploitation due to their fear of being detected and deported to their home countries involuntarily, that violates the customary rule of non-refoulement and other human rights principles. A common feature of the region vis-à-vis this category of people is that they often are used as vote banks by the political parties. Another serious consequences of forced migration is the programme of the host countries for their settlement in any area/s while balancing the host state's modernization programmes. Very often the land acquisition policy becomes difficult to balance the opposing interests of these different stakeholders. On the other hand, within the home state the remaining population belonging to the group fleeing their homes are faced with exclusion policy of the state and the consequent human rights violations. A common global and South Asian concern is also for refugee and stateless women and children becoming easy subjects of international trafficking. While such a condition requires state responsibility to adopt a clear cut regulation more often these cases are dealt with concern for spread of fatal diseases than from human rights of women and children.

While ethnic cleansing, torture and fear continues to force people cross borders, the states fearing refugee deluge continue evolving ways to restrict such forced flights. The sum total is the non-implementation of human rights regime for the 'people of concern'. Such situations often serve as potential ground for violence and other disruptive activities. Any approach or solution requires to be comprehensive and well-equipped to address all aspects of the issue, viz. from the causes of mass exodus to the mechanism of handling the refugee situations and their rehabilitation/repatriation. These functions are presently being undertaken by respective states. There is now increasing focus on political and economic conditions of countries of origin of refugees. While most of the acknowledged that human rights are interdependent to include not only civil and political rights but also economic, social and cultural rights, respect for all these rights is the necessary condition for the attainment of human development and the preservation of human dignity and gradual disappearance of refugee generating conditions. The positive similarities in the conditions prevailing in South Asia may offer mechanism for these exercises.

## Regime for Refugees

A survey of *international legal instruments* relating to the protection of life and dignity of human beings falling under different categories provides the following instruments that have both rights and duties of states and individuals/groups. They include, inter alia, Universal Declaration of Human Rights, Charter of the United Nations, Human Rights Covenants, Convention against Torture and Other Cruel, Inhuman Treatment or Punishment, Convention Relating to the Protection of Civilians in Time of War and the Additional Protocol, Convention relating to the Status of Stateless Persons, Convention on the Prevention and Punishment of the Crime of Genocide, Convention on the Elimination of all Forms of Discrimination against Women, Convention on the Rights of Child, etc. These instruments provide the following indivisible and interrelated rights to the refugees:

(i) right to seek and enjoy asylum from persecution;

(ii) right for non-refoulement if the return poses threat to life;

(iii) freedom of movement including freedom to choose his or her residence, freedom to leave any country, including his or her own and to return to his or her country;

(iv) right to non-discrimination based on race, colour, gender, language, religion, nationality, ethnicity, or status including protection from torture or ill-treatment;

(v) right to equal protection of the law including freedom from arrest or arbitrary or prolonged detention;

(vi) right to a nationality;

(vii) right to life including freedom from genocide and "ethnic cleansing" as well as adequate standard of living, including adequate food, shelter and clothing;

(viii) right to work;

(ix) right to live in a healthy and safe environment;

(x) right to education;

(xi) right to protection from economic and sexual exploitation, particularly for women, the aged and children;

(xii) right to freedom of association and demonstration; and

(xiii) right to peace and development.

Alongside these rights, the 1951 UN Convention relating to the Status of Refugees and the 1967 Protocol had set out principles and standards for the treatment of refugees. According to the Convention, the term *refugee* applies to any person who "as a result of events occurring before 1 January, 1951 and owing to well-founded fear of being persecuted for reasons of race, religion, nationality, membership of a particular social group or political opinion, is outside the country of his nationality and is unable, or owing to such fear, is unwilling, to avail himself of the protection of that country; or who, not having a nationality and being outside the country of his former habitual residence as a result of such events, is unable or, owing to such fear, is unwilling to return to it". The Convention had set the minimum standards of treatment of refugees, by emphasizing the fundamental rights that they may enjoy. It established the legal status of refugees along with their rights to employment, access to social welfare and other legal services, transfer of property, etc. in the host countries. The Convention also internationally recommended the naturalization and assimilation of refugees as lawful citizens in the host countries.

The Convention made the principle of *Non-refoulement* a non-derogable principle of international law signifying state responsibility not to return or expel persons to territories where they would face persecution and violence. In addition to these, the Convention made way to the humanitarian assistance to be provided by international bodies like the UNHCR. (In its resolution 319 A (IV) of 3 December 1949, the General Assembly decided to establish the Office of the United Nations High Commissioner for Refugees.) The Office was set up as a subsidiary organ of the General Assembly in January 1951. The Office of the UNHCR is located in Geneva, and functions in many countries. According to the Statute of the UNHCR, the main tasks are:

(i) to provide international protection to refugees by establishing camps;

(ii) to seek durable solutions for refugees by assisting governments to facilitate voluntary repatriation of refugees; and

(iii) their integration into the host country population.

The 1967 Protocol extended the application of the Convention to newer refugee generating situations applicable persons who, while meeting the Convention definition, had become refugees as a result of events that took place after 1 January 1951.

The *regional response* to the international refugee regime brought out Bangkok Declaration in 1966, the OAU Convention in 1969, the Cartagena Declaration in 1984. All these instruments expanded the definition of refugees in the changed circumstances of the respective regions and provided wider meaning of refugee. SAARC Law has also contributed substantially to developing model national legislation for refugees. SAARC Law, a regional body recognised by SAARC, brought together national associations of judges, legal administrators, academics and lawyers called for framing national legislations before formulating a regional instrument.

The ethnic and religious conflicts of South Asia and continued violence and denials of human rights alongside the prevailing inter-state relations, made refugee rights and human rights protection issue of these vulnerable groups take a less prioritized foreign policy issue for each South Asian country. However, two significant legal instruments require mention. The UNHCR after few informal consultations with academics, jurists, human rights activists brought out a Draft Model National Law on Refugees with a view to evolve comprehensive strategies to contain forced migration and human rights violations creating refugee conditions. The proposed Draft Model expanded the definition of refugee, including 'any person who owing to external aggression occupation, foreign domination, serious violation of human rights or other events seriously disrupting public order in either whole or part of his or her country of origin, is compelled to leave his or her place of habitual residence in order to seek refuge in another place outside his or her country of origin'. The draft law also recognized principle of non-refoulement as well as proposal for setting up of an independent refugee committee by the respective states. More importantly, the draft lays down procedures to determine refugee status while suggesting strategies to deal with situations of mass immigration and delineating refugee rights and duties for the ultimate objective to establish peace and conditions of equity and development. Beside this effort, the South Asian Forum for Human Rights invited different stakeholders to review refugee generating situations in South Asia, who emphasized on the need for developing regional instrument for outlining state responsibility vis-à-vis the refugees and other displaced persons. Recommendations for South Asia Protocol Charter for the Protection of Refugees, Migrants, Internally Displaced and Stateless Persons called on the states to create a regional protocol for the determination of the status of refugees and displaced persons.

The refugees in South Asia continue to face serious human rights problems right from the time of mass exodus to forcible repatriation and rehabilitation. None of the South Asian countries have ratified the 1951 Convention though the definition of the Convention is often applied in terms of such people crossing the border. In most cases no South Asian country have cohesive refugee law and policy with an amount of ad-hocism in dealing with the refugees. On the other hand, the countries of South Asia are known for providing shelter to the refugees. The dilemma remains as to how to balance these tendencies vis-à-vis the refugee problem.

The national scenario of refugee regime is more a cause for concern. With reference to India not a party to 1951 Convention, it adopted general principles of non-refoulement and the definition of refugee as per the Convention. At the same time, there is a lack of national policy which often results in non-recognition of refugees entering the Indian territory. The reasons for such a policy perhaps is guided by the geo-politics of South Asia alongside its international legal obligation. The Indian Constitution makes a mention of the entry and regulation of foreigners under the Union List by which the Central Government is empowered to deal with refugee issues. The Directive Principles of state policy mentions the fact that international law is not incorporated in Indian Municipal Law which is binding upon the state. India also did not adopt any policy for the determination of a refugee status. Most of the time the regulation of foreigners is based upon Foreigner's Act, the Foreigner's Order and the Illegal Migrants Determination Tribunals Act, 1983 (IMDT Act). This Act provides for the identification and deportation of such illegal migrants who entered into India on or after the 25 March 1971. On the other hand, India's ratification of the International Human Rights Instruments obliges India to apply equality and non-discrimination to its citizens and non-citizens (e.g. the refugees) as the minimum standards of human rights guarantees. The legal scenario of Bangladesh, Sri Lanka, Pakistan and Bhutan is similar to that of India. This make South Asia a very sensitive region where refugee generating conditions continue to prevail and where population fleeing their homes are acknowledged as refugees on an ad hoc basis only. Many a times one may observe that most of the South Asian countries not excluding India have accommodated the refugees who have been assimilated with the local population but officially they are yet to be treated as important subjects of international human rights.

Any regime for the protection of refugees requires appropriate procedures, rights and duties of all parties, institutions and financial capability. Lack of adequate legislation of any individual country on refugees and other such groups has compounded the problem of resolving this serious humanitarian issue.

The foregoing highlights clearly indicate that the protection regime for the refugees was created with a view to save those fleeing their homes under threats to their lives. But the changing global politics linked refugee protection regime with that of broader security regime making way to states often expressing their reluctance to provide shelter to the refugees. Thus, human rights violations of the refugees and other such vulnerable groups include: Violations of human rights as origins of mass exodus. In 1982, the Special Rapporteur presented his report to the Commission on Human Rights stating that "It is abundantly clear that unless ways can be found to counteract the withholding, of, or outright violations of, human rights, unless there is a more equitable sharing of the world's resources, more restraint and tolerance, the granting to everyone, regardless of race, religion, membership of a particular social group or political party, the right to belong or alternatively to move in an orderly fashion to seek work, decent living conditions and freedom from strife the world will continue to have to live with the problem of mass exodus." This problem, if left unchecked, will increasingly pose a threat to peace and stability around the globe. Perhaps the United Nations Department of Political Affairs calls for early warning activities in refugee generating countries to contain fresh flows of refugees on the one hand and strengthen monitoring and responding strategies and mechanism for refugees and displaced persons on the other. By 1992, a representative of the Secretary-General also highlighted the need for examining existing human rights, humanitarian and refugee laws and standards for the internally displaced persons, economic dimensions. One important function of this mechanism would be the monitoring of situations with a view to detecting early signs of displacement; Violations of the rights to life, liberty and security whereby refugees are made subject to attacks and ill treatment. Deaths in refugee camps due to armed attacks, recruitment in illegal armed groups are common to refugees; *Violations of refugee rights in the host countries* are a major cause of forced migration. The policy of adopting stringent immigration laws and non-availability of minimum rights of asylum-seekers in conditions of internal tensions in the refugee receiving countries alongside the refugee generating conditions in the countries of origin, are increasing. One may refer to women who constitute a large proportion of the world's refugee population and subjected to physical abuses.

The consequences are: the refugee generating conditions continue to prevail; the principle of non-refoulement has been repeatedly violated; the refugees continue to face violent reactions; the refugee issue has become more a political than a human rights concern; ad hocism in refugee policy still guides the states in South Asia. As long as violations of human rights persist in countries of origin, it is doubtful whether any refugee would decide to return voluntarily. Hence, the restoration of respect for and the promotion of all categories of human rights and the cessation of violent conflict in countries of origin are the necessary conditions for the voluntary return of refugees.

## The Way Ahead

The continuing political, social, economic and ethnic tensions act as the major cause of transborder population movements and refugee generating situations in South Asia. The receiving states are becoming much more cautious of the political, social, economic, strategic and environmental consequences of such movements of people. In addition to these, the post-Cold War restrictive immigration and asylum policies of a number of industrialized countries have made the developing countries wary of the consequences of hosting refugee population which in many occasions often leads to questioning the host state's human rights protection measures upholding international principles of refugee protection.

The discussion above indicates the reality of South Asia, where no refugee specific formal framework exists for addressing refugee problems at the national or regional levels. The ad hocism in dealing with the refuge seeking people often is arbitrary and discriminatory giving more space to the 'push-pull' syndrome. Moreover, application of numerous national Acts on the asylum-seekers often leads to confusion in identification and protection of refugees/asylum-seekers/stateless/illegal immigrants, etc. in the right manner. The most important reason perhaps, lies in the political conditions prevailing in

South Asia whereby only bilateral agreements are reached between the countries in a given situation. These conditions can be made better under the given scenario:

- All the South Asian states enact legislations for different categories of population crossing borders as asylum-seekers, stateless, illegal emigrants, etc. Such concrete laws would help identify conditions generating large influx of which category of people. The Acts would also indicate measures within the capability of a state to be adopted for each group people. The Acts would not apply several Acts together on these groups of people. Mention may be made of the application of IMDT Act or Foreigners' Acts in the NE India on the immigrant population and creation of volatile conditions thereafter. Finally human rights guarantees can be made more available if there are clearly demarcated laws at the national level for all the categories of people. This way the existing apprehensions that refugees are aiding and abetting terrorism and making military security issue more urgently to be addressed.
- The entire South Asia though faced with refugee generating conditions is yet to evolve refugee specific regional laws. The exercise of evolving and adopting regional refugee laws would help in many ways. First, the countries with numerous commonalities can identify divergences in their development programmes alongside their national interests. Secondly, the civil strifes and the deprivations acting as refugee generating conditions can be better addressed. Thirdly, cross border movements can become more lawful in place of the existing push-pull syndrome by each country. Fourthly, durable solutions, based on existing South Asian realities, for the refugees/stateless and illegal immigrants can be worked out more comprehensively. Finally, regional arrangements would also help furtherance of human rights for these people.

- The continued process of restricting immigration (principle of non-entree) alongside the promotion of temporary protection regimes as against the principle of non-refoulement and durable solution, has serious consequences for the working of international refugee regime as the institution of asylum. While the region is accommodating several thousand refugees, the need for refugee regime at the international level remains urgent for valid reasons. On the one hand, any violation of international refugee regulating principles by any state can draw international attention demanding resolution and restraint on state behaviour and evolution of harmonious policies related to several aspects of refugee problem on the other. Moreover, there will be opportunities to put Third World pressure while formulating international norms for durable solution of the problem.
- An important development since 2005, in the protection of refugees' life is the adoption and circulation by the UNHCR of Standards and Indicators for the protection of the refugees as people of concern for better implementation and management of these groups. Probably these features could bring in harmoniously implementable legal regime for the refugees, the stateless and the internally displaced people.
- The UN MDGs are formulated for the humanity's welfare in the next century. Evidently they are also applicable to refugees/stateless, IDPs, returnees, etc. Moreover, the Human Development Indices are meant for the overall development of humanity as a whole. The state are therefore to create conditions that would secure human development as part of fulfilment of MDGs by all states. These are the important changes that are gradually taking place in recent years. These changes are expected to help contain forced migration and refugee generating conditions in any region.

The challenge therefore lies in balancing the international, regional, national and local levels of protection mechanism for these people of concern so that they enjoy every rights that are human rights.

## REFERENCES

International Conventions.

Human Developments Reports.

The South Asia Declarations on Refugees, EPG.

World Refugee Survey.

Owen Nicholas. *Human Rights and HumanWrongs,* OUP, 2002.

Bose, Tapan and Rita Manchanda ed.; States, Citizens and Outsiders: The Uprooted Peoples of South Asia, South Asia Forum for Human Rights, Kathmandu, 1997.

Janusz Symondes. Human Rights: International Protection, Monitoring, Enforcement, UNESCO, 2005.

Lama, Mahendra. *Managing Refugees in South Asia* by, Occasional Paper 4, Refugee and Migratory Movements Research Unit, Dhaka, 2000.

Abrar, C.R. and Shahdeen Malik ed. *Towards National Refugee Laws in South Asia,* Refugee and Migratory Movements Research Unit, Dhaka, 2000.

Bose, Tapan. *Protection of Refugees in South Asia Need for Framework*, SAFHR Paper Series 5, South Asia Forum for Human Rights, Kathmandu.

Chimni, B.S. *The Law and Politics of Regional Solution of the Refugee Problem: The Case of South Asia*, RCSS Policy Studies 4, Regional Centre for Strategic Studies, Colombo, 1998.

# Problems of Human Rights as Reflected in Folk Literature of Bengal: Focus on Folk Songs in Particular

9

*Tathagata Chakraborty*

## I

Rights as a concept emerged in the 16th and 17th centuries as an opportunity to be enjoyed by the people as God-gifted or inherited from the nature which later on assumed legal implications with the emergence of the modern state. In the literature of modern social and political philosophy, one may find ample writings on rights. On the one hand, the Positivists maintain that the only genuine right is a claim which can be enforced and that any other account of a right is entirely subjective and metaphysical, on the other hand, certain rights are regarded to be moral rights which cannot be established by reference to an ongoing legal system but depend for their validity on their consistency with social and moral practices and on how they can be morally justified. Human rights or natural rights are regarded as types of moral right in that they do not depend for their validity on enforcement by the legal system but they are a special sort of moral right in that they do not emanate from specific promises or agreements, but are said to belong to all persons irrespective of what nation, community or social practice they may be a member of.[1] And same principle was followed when after the horrifying experience of two world wars, the United Nations General Assembly made a Declaration on Human Rights in 1948 saying that 'All human beings are born free and equal in dignity and rights. They are endowed with reason and conscience and should act towards one another in a spirit of brotherhood', this Declaration was no longer a legal binding upon the member-states of the United Nations. It was simply an appeal to their member-states to promote a number of human, civil, economic and social rights, asserting these rights are part of the foundation of freedom, justice and peace of the world. So it appears that there is a difference between rights and human rights in the sense that while rights imply legal connotation, human rights refer to those rights which may or may not have legal connotation but it has to be humane in nature. It is to be mentioned here that there are certain moral rights which have been incorporated in the constitutions of certain states and there is always a hue and cry to include certain moral rights within the legal framework and nowadays human rights as a concept has assumed a different connotation.

Keeping all these in mind, we shall try to peep into a small segment of a vast Bengali folk literature and try to focus on certain glaring examples which express their concern about certain human rights: the right to life and liberty, freedom of thought and expression and equality before the law. Apparently, they may appear innocuous. But a careful observation may interpret that they talk about certain social issues which come under the periphery of human rights. In this way, the problem of dowry, child marriage, the agony of an unhappy marriage, the bondage of women, persecution by the mother-in-law, sister-in-law or the husband, economic exploitation in various forms are reflected in these examples which sometimes are quite apparent and sometimes expressed subtly.

## II

As we know, folklore is a tradition based on any expressive behaviour that brings a group together, creates a convention and commits to a cultural memory of the given society; one may carve out the state of mind or the thought process of the common folk by analysing various elements of folklore. At the outset, we shall try to mention some types of Bengali folk literature.

They are:

(a) Folk tales
(b) proverbs and adage
(c) vow
(d) ballad and folksongs.

Now we shall try to cite certain examples to elaborate the ideas.

**Folk Tales**

Folk tales include fairy tales, legend, metaphorical story, allegorical story, mythological story, etc. These stories are simple. There are certain characters which are either good or bad. There are various interactions among these characters. However, at the end of the story good always prevails over the bad. But among all these stories, one can find out certain patterns, e.g. the story of a king who has beloved queen (suyorani) and hated queen (duorani). While suorani plays lot of tricks for which duorani has to suffer a lot. But ultimately by the stroke of fate, duorani comes closer to the king and suorani is served rightly. If we see the list of the atrocities which are being made upon duorani throughout the story, we may find how severely human rights are denied to duorani.

There is another story: Saat Bhai Champa (seven brothers and their sister). The story goes like this: step-mothers out of jealousy buried seven sons and one daughter of duorani in a dump of ashes. After some days, a tree sprouted on that spot which had seven Champak flowers and one trumpet (parul) flower. But no one could touch those flowers until and unless duorani, the mother came to rescue them. And finally, the step-mothers were severely punished. From this story particularly, one signal is quite apparent, i.e. the abuse made by the step-mother towards her step-children in the society.

In all these stories, we find two types of conflict: (a) in one side the king, queen, prince, princess and on the other hand demons (rakshasa-khokkasa), magician, witch, supernatural power and (b) in one side common poor, good men like farmer, weaver, fisherman, barber and on the other side the king, queen, prince, princess who are either bad or/and rich. In both cases, ultimately wins the humanity and the goodness. One may assume that these stories in some cases are stories of wishful thinking as in reality they do not occur always.

## Vow

Vow ('bratakatha') is a form of rites/custom usually performed on various occasions by womenfolk. Practice of each vow is associated with some sort of achieving both celestial and worldly pursuits. Womenfolk on some particular days as in most cases mentioned in almanac, exercise certain rites, worship in most cases without Brahmins or priests. Finally, they pronounce certain riddles something like sacred hymns which are self-explanatory of their desire.

Let us have some examples of those vow and their corresponding riddles:

**Tush-tushuli Brata:** Performed in Bengali month Pousha (mid-December to mid-January) having a desire for the prosperity of father's as well as father-in-law's house. One of the riddles of this vow is: [*Ghar korbo nagare/morbo giye sagare/janmabo uttam kuliner ghare,*] I shall stay at the town/I shall die at the sea/I will be reborn in the house of well-to-do high rank (kulin) Brahmins. It explains that women suffer miserably in the village so wants to stay at a town; and the life of a girl is miserable who does not have a high pedigree to be married to a kulin family.

**Dash Puttal Brata:** Performed in Bengali month Baishakha (mid-April to mid-May) having a desire of attaining both celestial and worldly prosperity. One of the riddles of this vow is: [*ebar moley manush habo/Brahman kule janmo labo*]. After my death, I wish to be born as male in a Brahmin family. This riddle also harps on the same tune that is to be born in a non-Brahmin family moreover as a female is a curse. It explains the poor position of lower caste women in our society.

**Senjuti Brata:** This is performed in the evening throughout the month of Agrahayana (mid-November to mid-December) with the intention to get blessings for all the family members so that all of them may prosper. These riddles express the simple desire of the womenfolk. But in some expressions surface the day-to-day sufferings of them where they are deprived of basic human rights. Following are the examples:

- [*ashathatalay baash kori/Satin kete aalta pori*] I stay under the peepul tree/paint the borders of my feet by the co-wife's blood stains (killing her).
- [*Satin hok dashi/aami dekhe hoi khushi*] Let the co-wife become the maid servant/and I become happy.
- [*kanta, kanta, kanta/Satin ke maari jhanta*] Co-wife is like a thorn/I should beat her with broomstick.

It is quite known that there was an accepted system in Indian family to have more than one wife. Sometimes, particularly in the case of kulin Brahmins, it could be more than hundred. Among them, some one is dearer to the husband. Others may not have same kind of attachment for which they were treated discriminately. So to get married to a husband who is already married is regarded to be a misfortune as it begets domestic violence, outrageous activities of both husband and his beloved and honoured wife over less liked wives. It has been mentioned earlier in fairy tales, the story of duorani and suorani which again is an illustration of domestic violence even under the garb of the story of the king and the queen. These examples stand testimony to the gloomy side of the society where there is domestic violence by the husband, co-wives, in-laws and parents, unequal treatment over caste identity. In the discussion of the following sections, we will also find the reflection of the same social evils where people are deprived of human rights miserably.

## Proverbs and Adage

A proverb is a traditional saying which offers advice or presents a moral in a short and pithy manner, while adage refers to a saying often in a metaphorical form that embodies a common observation. In both cases they are expressed as riddle or so. Some examples are:

- [*jate tate dao bor, duo jak satiner ghar*] In any case, please give me some boon, so that the disliked girl may have a co-wife.
- [*bimata bisher ghor*] The home with step-mother is a curse.

- [*uthte lathi, boste kil*] When you stand up, you get a kick, if you sit down, you get a blow.
- [*Kanyar maa kande aar takar puntli bandhe*] Mother cries at the time of daughter's marriage and at the same time accumulates money for dowry.
- [*Kaar khailam dhcrkarja, kaar goilam churi/kane ba lagailen more jailkhanar dori/jailkhanar chaardike paoror dewal/taar moidhey bandhi raakhe/monisher chawal*] I do not know for whom I have taken loan or stolen other's property/or why I have been taken to jail/the jail has got four walls with stone/And men are kept in that jail.

Now, the first one suggests the cursed plight in a home with co-wives. The second one delineates the atrocity by step-mother. The third one talks about the tragedy of the mother in connection with the system of dowry. The fourth one tells about the perpetual torture upon the bride at the in-law's house. The fifth one in the form of a riddle depicts the day-to-day sufferings of a person who does not know about his mistakes. It appears as if this world is something like a jail and he has been put up there as a criminal. These expressions are candid and unintentional. They are not designed to make any protest. Neither did they have before them any political authority to make appeal and express their sorrow and sufferings nor to make protest for reparation. And conspicuously those may be considered as candid expression in the vocabulary of common man's literature. Now let us turn into some other form in the next section.

## III

### Folk Songs

I like to turn our attention to some examples from the rich tradition of Bengali folk songs and ballads to illustrate the same. As mentioned earlier, in most cases these songs cannot be typified as protest songs as they are neither aimed at any political authority nor they speak about any conscious struggle against unjust social order. But they express their day-to-day misery and grief in a candid manner and consider their condition as a stroke of ill luck though some of the scholars are of the opinion that 'In a broader sense a good number of our love songs, marriage songs or songs known as Baramashay, Biraha or Dehotattva, etc. express in an indirect way a protest against the social system.'[2] Of course it is true that those songs were composed and sung in a patriarchal, semi-feudal, caste-ridden, conservative society where in some social groups polyandry was officially an accepted norm (where males can have officially more than one wives and co-wives called each other Satin) but at the same time, people were confused about there social position and in most cases they could not make out any solution. Those atrocities reflected in these songs no doubt talked about the denial of human rights to the common folk but appeared before us in the form of sigh and weep. We present here some of those examples.

The following is an example of Chatka song (Bhawaia) of North Bengal. This song particularly is sung in a lighter vein. But it reflects how men cheat women who face the distress after marriage.

*Naak-dangrar byatata, chouk dangrar natita/*
*mook bhulalu sater kharu dia !*
*Takhani na kachish tui Re/Haal charikhan goru paanch hal*
*Cheuti gorur nekhaijokai nai/Ore, bari aashia dekhnu mui*
*Chaturali korlu tui/Gharot hina tor chaane dibar nai!*
*Takhan na kochish tui re/Mota chaul khai naa*
*Soru chauler lekhaijokai nai/Ore bari aashia dekhon mui*
*Chaturali korlu tui/Gharot hina tor khudir gurao nai!*
*Takhani na kachish tui re/Mota kapor pindhi na, soru kaporer Nekhaijokai nai*
*Ore bari aashia dekhon mui*
*Chaturali korlu tui/Barite tor phara taani nai!*
*Takhani na kachish tui Re/Domahala temahala tiner gharer nekhaijokai nai/Ore bari aashia dekhon mui*
*Chaturali korlu tui/Gao garebar bichna na pang mui!*

[You shameless man—You have cheated me with toys!

Before marriage, you said, you have four ploughs, innumerable cows/But as I entered your house after

marriage, I find that you don't have even straws at the rooftop!
Before marriage, you said, you take only fine rice and unable to take coarse rice;
But as I entered your house after marriage, I find that you don't have even fragment of grain!
Before marriage, you said, you take only fine clothing and you have a big collection of garments.
But as I entered your house after marriage, I find that you don't have even a piece of rag!
Before marriage, you said, you have two-storied/three-storied house with tin-rooftop!
But as I entered your house after marriage, I find that you don't have even a space for a bed!]

These marriages in most cases involve the system of dowry. This dowry is of two types. In the first case, the dowry is demanded from the groom's family and in the case of a poor father it creates pressure on him thereby the poor father has to either sale off their belongings or take loan from the rich people at a high interest and subsequently falls into a recurring financial crisis. In the second case, the groom is to pay money to the bride's family. In that case, the poor father arranges marriage of his daughter to a groom who is not a proper match. The distress is stretched at the in-law's house and it appears to the girl that her father has sold her out in the name of marriage for handful of money. The expression (Baacheya khaiche) means reverse dowry where the groom is to offer dowry to the bride's family. In the Goalparia song of Assam we find this kind of statement:

*Oki o mor bhaber daora*
*Thuiya aay mok bapre bhaiyar daashe;*
*Baapo bhai mor durachar*
*Baacheya khaiche mok durantare*
*Baacheya khaiche mok ganjaruar ghare!*
*Ganjarua ganja khay*
*Aagun dite mor raati pohay re*
*Naathir dange mor sharir hoilo kalare!*

[Oh my younger brother-in-law/please send me to my father's house. Both my father and brother are wicked persons. They have sold me far way off! My husband is a ganja-smoker/I am to supply fire for his smoking. He also beats me black and blue with stick!]

In some other songs, we find similar expressions:

*Madokia mado khaya/mor paranta jwaliya jay* [My husband is a drunkard. The whole night he goes on drinking and my life becomes miserable].

*Guachatay gua khay/mor paranta jwaliya jay* [My husband is a betel-taker. The whole night he goes on taking betel and my life becomes miserable].

*haichat thakiya basnu biya o / kaoner bhater aashe*

*ela dhano nai, chaulo nai/ kilay mashe mashe* [Though I was a widow, still I got married for the second time just for food. But instead of getting full meal, I get only beatings and thrashings].

In another Goalparia song, a tragic situation is described where a girl was married or sold to a boy who is still a baby. At night she finds that her baby husband in a state of sleepiness addresses her as 'mother'.

*Mon mor kandey re/rati nishaor kaalere*
*Nindiar alashe pati mor maa boliya daake.*
*Aarey baapu kana/Ma o kaana o*
*daaruno bidhi kana parar log*
*Paishar lobhe bechiya khaisay*
*Suwami nabalok mon mor kande re!*
*Arey koi ya dane moor doyal babako*
*Kanga muk dudho khai ye kanga moor*
*Pati manush hoibay/mon mor kandere!*

[My mind weeps at night, when in his half sleep my baby husband calls me mother. Oh! my father is blind and my mother too. And it is my fate that the neighbors also chose to be blind. The want of money has prompted them to sell me off. Since my husband is an infant, ask my father to send me some milk so that after drinking that milk, he may attain manhood].

As we were centering round our discussion, we should refer to those songs related to the system of kulin marriage that brought forth the denial of human rights to innumerable poor

Brahmin kulin[3] girls. One can get a number of writings on this subject in our literature including folk songs. An interesting reference can be traced in a collection of folk songs in Bengali, 'Prachin PurbaBanga Gitika', Vol. IV edited by Kshitish Chandra Moulik. In this collection he referred to *Bharar Meyer Gaan,* meaning a particular type of songs associated with the marriage of kulin girls. In monsoon times in East Bengal, a group of matchmakers used to come to the villages to collect kulin Brahmin unmarried girls mainly from the poor kulin families and take them out silently at night in a large boat (the boat was nicknamed as *Bharar nouka*) towards unknown destination with a promise to their fathers that those girls would be given marriage to kulin bridegrooms. In most cases, those girls were either married to non-kulins or they were sent to Vaishnava Goswamis. A huge transaction of dowry was made for this out of which a big slice would go to the village heads. Thus, a good number of kulin girls were forced to live either as beggar or had to submissively accept prostitution.

There are certain songs on this theme. Some examples are:

> *Sheo she aamar chilo bhalo/hay re bidhata na sohilo/ Nishi raitey bharar naye/more aakule bhashailo* [It was better to remain alone. But God could not allow me the grace; as I was at night deported to unknown destination by the bharar nao (the boat).]
>
> *Aami to abala nari/ aamar kichu koibar nai/chokher jol aanchale muichhay Sayare bhaisahya jai* [I am a helpless girl, I have got nothing to do. So I only shed tears and had to flow down the sea.]

The system of child marriage is also connected with the system of kulin marriage, which stands as glaring example of denial of human rights. It is true that child marriage was not confined only to the high caste kulins but also popular among the low-caste people. Even today this system still continues. However, though there were several attempts to stop this practice right from the days of Iswarchandra Vidyasagar, but there was a serious attempt in 1929 when a legislative Act was passed in Legislative Assembly of India making the minimum age of marriage 14 years for girls. It involved British and Indian social reformers on the issue of marriage. Marriage affected the majority of population and involved all communities and this was the first legislation to impose a minimum age for marriage. This Act is popularly known as Sarda Act. The Act was passed in September 1929 and came into effect in April 1930. Within this period, from mid-November to mid-April, a huge number of girls were married off to even old haggard just because the marriage of girl child before her puberty was considered to be religiously sacrosanct. Controversy over the acceptability of the issue continued among the religious leaders and the social reformers throughout the country. Interestingly enough we can also cite two examples one in favour and another against the Act.

In Kolkata, in a farcical song popularly known as *Jeleparar Shang*, we find that they did not approve the Act and therefore they composed a satirical song against the passing of the Act.

> *Biye noy thakurpujo soja chelekhela/bor-koner chokher koney mon-mojano mela.*
> *(tai) na uthle palak, na-balokke biye dile/shunchi bisham bhul*
> *Biye biye kore jakhan meye sabe pagol/takhon tare dhore debe jutiye ekta chagol*
> *Na hole gol badhabe Harabilash/daroga dekhabe rule*

[Marriage is not a simple religious act. It is interplay of eyes between bride and the groom. If the boy is not mature enough, it is wrong to make a boy groom.

But when the girl becomes mad for getting married, then people shall provide with a goat. Otherwise, Harabilash shall create trouble and the police will come and show you rule!]

But just opposed to this sentiment, there is a reflection of the same issue in a Bhadu song of Radh area of Bengal:

> *Baro moja geche go aiin pashe goto phagun mashe.*
> *Hok na bura kana-khonra, jeno na tar gaal bashe,*
> *Cha bacharer sishuke diyeche sindur ghoshe!*
> *Bhalobashar katha chiloje/ paanchpayra punam sari*
> *Shange nei tor paishakari neche mon bhulali!*

[It is a great fun (!) that a law was passed for which a number of girls even if they were six years old were rubbed sindur (vermilion) on their forehead as a mark of marriage by old men even if they were blind or lame but not having shrunken face. It was expected to have gorgeously decorated saris as a mark of love. But instead the girl had to dance to capture her husband's mind as she did not have money.]

So far we have gone through the songs, the theme of which was dowry, child marriage, and domestic violence particularly by the in-laws. Now, we shall turn into some other examples which tell about social injustice, economic exploitation which is the other name of denial of human rights.

## IV

About hundred years back, coolies were brought into the tea gardens of Assam from the Chhotanagpur area of Bengal. These coolies had ideas that since they had a very poor living in their villages, the call for green tea plantation would improve their living. But in reality they had to experience the same exploitation if not more in Assam. Out of this experience a new type of folk song emerged as an admixture of Assamese tune and Jhumur songs of rahr Bengal. This type of song is known as *Cha Baganer Jhumur*. Here we shall mention two songs:

*Chol mini Assam jabo: deshe boro dukh re*
*Assam dese re mini Cha-bagan ghuria*
*sardar bole kam kam/babu bole dhorey aan*
*sahib bole nibo pither cham! O jaduram*
*phanki diya pathaili Assam*
*ek poisar puntimaach/pata tula kam go*
*minir baape mange jodi aroi dibo jhol go!*

[Let us, mini (addressing a girl) go to tea gardens in Assam for job, as the life in our native place (Chhotanagpur) is full of misery. But alas! In Assam there we find that the misery still continues. The leader of the coolies compels us to work more and more; and the Sahibs of tea gardens terrorise us that they would otherwise pull our skins out by beating. This dreaded experience is due to Jaduram, the agent of coolies who made false promise to bring us here. Our remuneration for plucking tea leaves is so meager that we can buy only small fish. If mini's father demands more food, he would have nothing but only the curry (without fish).]

*Mone kori Assam jabo/jora pankha tangaibo*
*Asamer Saheb dilo kodalia kam go!*
*He kalia Shyam/phanki diya pathaili Assam!*
*Tumi amar keba chile, amar dike takaile*
*Lal kalite likhaile saatpurusher naam!*
*Ekti duti katha bole kaam koaraili Dibrugore*
*Dibru dekhe urilo paran go!*

[I thought that I shall go to Assam and (become so rich) that I shall have two fans at a time at the roof. But the Sahib provided me with only the job of spade-work (instead of job at tea garden). Oh my beloved Krishna! You have cheated me by sending me to Assam!

You are none to me. But stared at me and wrote in red ink the names of our forefathers! You have cheated me by sending me to Assam. You spent only one or two words to make me work at Dibrugarh (Assam).]

These two songs possibly reveal the denial of basic human rights to the coolies of tea gardens.

## V

So far, we tried to focus on the texts of certain songs which talk about the denial of basic human rights to the common folk. But in this section, we like to focus on those singers who are being denied of human rights for their songs they sing or for the religion they follow. They are known as Bauls and Fakirs and their religion is clearly contradistinctive from the mainstream religion—both Hinduism and Islam. The attack comes from the conservative fundamentalists and this has become apparent almost from the emergence of Baul sect in early 17th century. And it still continues. To understand the reason, we are to look at the social history of the then Bengal.

As we know, a self-sufficient village, based on agriculture and handicrafts by means of simple instruments was the basic feature of pre-colonial Bengal. Socially it was dominated by Vedic vis-à-vis Brahmin culture. The society almost completely subordinated the individual to the caste, the family and the village panchayat, throughout its century-old existence. The village population continued to live the same sterile, superstitious, narrow, stereo-typed social and intellectual existence. The Hindus, comprising two-thirds of the population were almost atomized in various castes and sub-castes, a phenomenon peculiar to the Hindu society.[4] The very appearance of Chaitanya Deva (1476-1530) tried to wash out this caste barrier and establish a new egalitarian social order which again got a blow when the reactionary sections of the people brought back the caste system more forcefully in post-Chaitanya period. As a reaction to it, emerged a number of minor sects, protestant in character trying to defy the mainstream religious practices. Among those, the Bauls as a sect appeared in the year 1625. 'These unlettered village-singers, known as the Bauls, belong to the lower ranks of both the Muslim and the Hindu communities of Bengal and they are composed partly of householders and mainly of mendicants. The Bauls belonging to Hindu community are generally Vaisnavite in their faith and those belonging to Muslim community are generally Sufi-istic and in both the schools the emphasis in on the mystic conception of divine love.'[5] It developed as a syncretic cult influenced by Tantric Budhism, Shiva-Shakti cult, Vaishnavism, Sufi-ism and Vaishnava Sahajiya cult. It included primitive sexual rites, intricate yogic practices declaiming traditional lineage of any particular community. They maintained certain manners and customs, habits or practices, harped more and more on the emotions rather than ceremonious rituals. They consciously avoided the usual religious path and therefore neither they were liked nor approved by the mainstream religious leaders.

Possibly Professor Dasgupta wanted to mean the Fakirs as Sufiist. Though this kind of definition is not fully acceptable, but for the sake of the present article, I like to group Bauls and Fakirs within the same bracket as the problem is faced both by Bauls and Fakirs. Bauls got a lot of support from the common people. They rendered support while these Baul-fakirs stood at their doorstep for food grains, sing Baul songs and collect food grains by begging which was a part of their rites. People used to listen to their songs, copy them and sing as well. The emergence of Baul songs as a part of their religious activities was a later development (approximately in 1650). These songs were peculiar in nature having a typical style; the singers were always charged emotionally and the songs are sung mostly in a high pitch. Themes include some symbolic expressions as moner manush (man of heart), achin pakhi (unknown bird), bird and the cage, river, etc. An important part of these songs include *Dehatatwa* (Lore and cult of body)—the basic metaphysics of Baul. 'The respiratory air, the action of respite, the female reproductive organ, the monthly menstruation of women, the strange modus operandi of menstrual flux and semen-fluid consisting of respectively ovum and spermatozoa—termed as the archetypal water of creation; earth, water, air, fire, ether—the five elements of the universe and of course of human body—the body as the abode of *Atma* which is supposed to have the final communion with *Paramatma*, are the principal features of *Dehatatwa*—the key of human salvation in this mundane world.' These songs maintain symbolic expressions for which those always carry double meaning. Apparently to a layman, many of these songs convey simple devotional meaning but at the higher level it carries the secrets of their philosophy in the shelter of unintelligible symbols which does not have mainstream religious sanctions for which these Baul-Fakirs were socially ostracized. An example may illustrate present position:

> *Khelche maamush kshire-neere/apon apon ghor bojho aamar/keno hatre berao koler ghare? Shunya deshe megher uday, neerad bindu barishan tay/tate faleche fal rangberang hal aajob kudrati kal bhaber ghare* [Men are playing in water (menstrual flux) and on thicken milk (semen-fluid of men)/O my mind! Recognize your own home. With vision blurred why do you grope about in the darkness of your lap? In empty space (from the gray matter within the skull), cloud appears and drops down rain (emotion of creating life) Fruit of various hues grow strange creative skill in emotional level.]

Moreover, in their songs they questioned the fundamental principle of caste and religious divisions existing in the society which is solely created by man himself. Certain examples from the composition of Lalon Fakir is as follows:

- *Jat gelo Jat gelo boley eki aajab Karkhana/ satyapathe keu noy raji, shabi dekhi ta-na-na-na* [They say, I shall be excommunicated/This sounds queer to me/None willing to follow justice, Everybody shilley-shallies.]
- *Sabloke koy Lalon ki jat sanshare? Lalon bolet jatir kirup dekhlam e najore/Chunnyat dile hoy mushalman/ tabe narir ki hoy bidhan/Bamun chini poitey proman/ bamni chini ki korey* [They want to ascertain to which religion Lalon belongs./Unfolded yet to be/the features are caste to me—says Lalon/Circumcision confirms one as a Muslim/What about a Muslim Woman?

A Brahmin is known by his sacred thread/How to recognise a Brahmin Lady?][6]

As it has been mentioned earlier, Bauls and Fakirs are being denied of human rights for their songs they sing or for the religion they follow. The blow basically comes from the social and religious elites for a number of reasons.

(i) It totally pushes aside the caste system and talks about the free mixing based on the philosophy of *Moner Manush* (man of the heart).

(ii) Its suggestion of promiscuous sex rites for *Sadhana*, popular among the tantrik practitioners, was never approved by socio-religious leaders.

(iii) It tried to give an alternative model of living that was regarded as major social taboo.

(iv) The crux of philosophy which interprets the body as microcosm of the universe is that the ultimate reality resides within the human form as our true self or the ultimate nature. So it is always necessary to search for the man of the heart nearby rather than to rush into temples, mosques and pilgrimages.

So, it becomes quite clear that philosophically it made protest against the religious institutions for which the religious leaders, particularly the fundamentalist segments, became furious and socially it decried the caste domination thereby making the social leaders fretful. Gradually, a section of the social and religious leaders pounced upon the Baul-Fakirs with vengeance to wash them out from the society. And the battle started.

'Bauls were persecuted both by Shariat Muslims and Hindu religious practitioners. This persecution has sometimes turned into torture. According to Muslims, they were termed as *beshra, bedati, nadar Fakir* and Hindus termed them as outcaste, loathsome, excommunicated persons....' Bauls became popular in 19th century. At the same time atrocity on them increased to a length. At the time of Wahabi, Farhazi and Ahale Hadish movement, the number of Bauls started decreasing. Many of the Bauls who were originally Muslims had to reconvert themselves to Islam via Shariat. Even at the time of the movement led by Titu Meer (1782-1831) Bauls were tortured. Munshi Mohammad Meherullah (1861-1907), the eminent Muslim intellectual undermined the Bauls as *stupid vedua* and their songs as Kaferi *Kalam*. Apart from these, a number of books and booklets against the Bauls were written. Lot of protest movements also took place against Lalan Fakir while he was alive.

In the year 1926, the second edition of the book *Baul Dhangsha Fatoah* was published.[7] It is true that the objective condition that paved the way to the emergence of the Bauls has changed though these songs are still highly valid particularly in the present context as the caste and religious barriers in our society have not been removed. The number of practicing Bauls is on the wane though the number of Baul singers is increasing day-by-day thanks to the media. They are basically performers who present themselves in the traditional attire. Songs are in most cases composed on modern issues and sometimes they even use modern musical instruments. The Baul singers of this category do not face any trouble as it happened in the 19th century rural Bengal. What is alarming is that a lot of incidents are nowadays taking place involving persecution of Baul-Fakirs in the rural Bengal. They are being treated in the same way as it occurred previously. The long hairs of the Baul-Fakirs are forcibly cut-off, sometimes they are beaten black and blue and socially boycotted. An investigation by an NGO[8] reveals that between 1973 and

2001, in three districts (Nadia, Birbhum and Murshidabad) of West Bengal at least there were fifty incidents where at least one hundred and fifty Baul-Fakirs faced severe atrocities. It may be assumed that this has been due to the recent reappearance of the fundamentalists in our country. Moreover, in this battle, in most cases they are intra-communal, that is, while Hindu fundamentalists aim at the Hindu liberals, the Muslim fundamentalists attack the Muslims liberals. Though it is true that there are uproars against this kind of attack from the various corners of the society, but how this problem is to be solved is yet to be seen.

## REFERENCES

*A few folk songs of Old Goalpara,* Wild Grass, Assam, 1999.

Basak, Shila, *Banglar Brata Parban,* Calcutta, 1998.

Bandopadhyay, Bireswar, Banglar Shong, Calcutta, 1996, 2nd edition.

Chakrabarti, Sudhir, *Baul-Fakir Katha,* Calcutta, 2001.

Chakrabarti, Bikash, Baul Jibaner Samajtatwa, Calcutta, 2003.

Dasgupta, Kali, Ki O Kajal Bhromara, Calcutta, 2005.

Giri, Satyabati, *Article: Bharar Meyer Gaan* in the journal Lkashangashkriti Gabeshana ed. Sanat K. Mitra, Vol. 9, No. 3, 1403 (Bangabda).

Pathan, Md. Hanif, Banglar Probad Parichiti: Vols. 1, 2 and 3, Dacca, 1976.

Mukherjee, Sumita, "Using the Legislative Assembly for Social Reform: The Sarda Act of 1929" in the *Journal South Asia Research*, Vol. 26930, pp. 219-33.

## NOTES

1. Hart, HLA: "Are There Only Natural Rights" in A. Quintin (ed) *Political Philosophy*, London, OUP.
2. Hemango Biswas, *A Glorious Heritage in Folkmusic and Folklore: An Anthology,* ed. by Hemango Biswas, Calcutta, 1967.
3. This system led to hypergamy where bridegroom must be from a higher caste or sub-caste resulting in surplus of unmarried girls. As sastras ordained that the daughters must be married off before puberty and pronounced curses on defaulters, one man married a large number of brides, who were never supported economically by the husband. Thus, marriage itself became a gainful occupation. Among the kulin brahmins, even septuagenarians and octogenarians, with two or three dozens of wives, were considered good matches by

the helpless parents of kulin brahmin girls. A kind of marriage fees, ranging from Rs. 5/- to Rs. 500/- was usually charged by the kulin brahmins for marrying a kulin girl. Even teenagers were married to dying octogenarian husbands. The old man's gain, before his death, was a few rupees—Ghose, Benoy, *Iswar Chandra Vidyasagar*, Publication Division, Govt. of India, 1965.

4. A.R. Desai, *Social Background of Indian Nationalism*, Bombay, 1976.
5. Sashibhushan, Dasgupta. *Obscure Religious Cult*, Calcutta, 1976.
6. Translations of Lalon songs by Nanigopal Ruidas, *Songs of Lalon Fakir*, Calcutta, 1997.
7. Abul Ahasan, Chowdhury. *Lalan Smarak Grantha*, Jatiya Granthakendra, Dacca, 1974.
8. Source: Shaktinath, Jha. *Baul-fakir Dhangsher Itibritta*, Calcutta, 2001.

# Science, War and Human Rights

*Syamal Chakrabarti*

10

We all know that the United Nations took some historical initiatives to formulate a number of articles (1 to 30) in order to protect human rights for mankind irrespective of gender, wealth, ethnicity and nationality. In 1998, United Nations organised a conference to observe fifty years of human rights where it adopted the statement "all human rights for all". The very essence of this statement clearly suggests that all kinds of people are not enjoying their legitimate rights effectively. In fact, these inequalities are quite often reflected by the series of events happening everyday in our planet. War is such an event when the basic principles of human rights are not implemented properly.

Let us now come to the basic question: What is war? It is a state of conflict, generally armed between two or more entities. In addition it is characterized by international violence on the part of large bodies of individuals organized and trained for that purpose. These two points are important.

The definition of war leads to another question: What is civil war? It has been pointed out that we are, at present, in a constant state of war. This statement must partly indicate a kind of civil war, which is described as 'war fought internally between rival political factions on national level'. These facts are well-known but they nevertheless provide a suitable basis for this discussion, as does the answer to the question of why wars are fought. The answer given is 'to protect religion/race/colour', which indicates an element of protection as well as of destruction. Thus, many wars are fought in the name of "Self defence". This also leads to increases in the defence budget of various countries in the name of national security. Wars are also waged 'to acquire territory or resource', and most relevant to this discussion, 'to spread political and ideological leadership'. Real wars have been fought and are being fought around us. Of these three are relevant to this discussion. One of them went on for nearly a hundred years—the Crusades, next the First World War, which lasted for five years, and the Second World War which continued for seven years, changed the world irrevocably.

The main issue here is to find out the part played and to be played in this vast expanse of war in civilization by science and scientists, whether such a part was at all desired or not desired, and how far such a role is conducive to the continued survival of the earth. For it is unquestionable that the advancement of civilization owes much if not all to science. True, there are negative shades to this progress but that is due to the way science has been used, not to science itself. Life without science would result in what may be called a civilization of cockroaches, for these creatures have been proved to be the only life-forms capable of surviving the most difficult physical conditions including radiation. There is, then, no denying of the major role of science and technology in providing the comforts and advantages that human beings at present enjoy. It is necessary, in this regard, to remember how science developed and technology came into being. There is one important thing about science. This can be seen in the manner in which, at the dawning of scientific awareness, rich men, interested in science maintained their personal laboratories at home. One example of this would be the renowned astronomer Sir Joseph Norman Lockyer. Another was Lord Rayleigh who counted Jagadish Chandra Bose as his outstanding pupil. Of all the papers published by Jagadish Chandra in the journal of the *Royal Society*, all but two were recommended by Lord Rayleigh (a research paper can be published in that journal only on the recommendation of another fellow of the Society). The name of a third scientist relevant to this discussion is Henry Cavendish, the discoverer of hydrogen, whose name is well-known. If one was asked to name the best scientist among wealthy men interested in science, or conversely, to name one of the wealthiest men who was interested in science, the answer to both questions would be Henry Cavendish. Cavendish was a very rich man but he was also a very eccentric man. He avoided speaking to women and women were not allowed to speak to him unless they veiled themselves in black. Of course someone like this could hardly lead a normal family life and Cavendish had none. He died, ensuring that his money would benefit students interested in science regardless of their race, nationality or creed. The University of Cambridge received endowments to build research centres. It will be found that most of the Nobel laureates in science worked at the Cavendish laboratories of Cambridge University. The names of these three scientists—Lockyer, Lord Rayleigh and Henry Cavendish—are noteworthy, for they belong to a time when neither science nor scientists received any form of assistance, material or otherwise from governments. Those who could afford it pursued scientific knowledge for no other reason than that they were driven to do so. How did this state of affairs change then?

Things changed around the time of the First World War, when a sort of arms race began between the countries involved, with each trying to make poisonous gases which would kill the most people. This is why, as history students know, the First World War is said to be one of chemical warfare, in which scientists, irrespective of their nationality, out of xenophobia, jingoism or patriotism, conducted extensive research in laboratories to synthesize poisonous chemicals. There was a time when national governments felicitated scientists according to the number of people the gases they created could kill. In other words, the greater a scientist's contribution to his or her governments' ability to massacre humans, the greater the respect he earned. Scientists worldwide then, moved from a position in which they were obliged to conduct research out of their personal interest to a position in which governmental support was provided for the first time. A discussion of the part played by scientists in the Second World War would be a very long one, and therefore will be restricted to only one aspect of it—the project of Los Alamos where scientists who had fled from Europe gathered to create the nuclear bomb in 1945. It was tested on an island on the 16th of July. Oppenheimer, the scientist who was also a

Sanskrit scholar, quoted a *shloka* saying that if any other human had seen the horror he had witnessed, that person would never be involved in any wrongdoing again. It is worth mentioning that Hiroshima-Nagasaki had not yet happened. A committee of experts formed by scientists headed by James Frank urged that the nuclear bomb not be tested on humans for they felt that human life would be of as little value as the beasts if the bomb was used on them. Scientists from various fields, such as Oppenheimer, J.D. Bernal, Linus Pauling or Albert Einstein were all deeply involved in the scientific research for the First or Second World War. Fritz Haber is famous for the synthesis of Ammonia from nitrogen and hydrogen. Haber had produced a number of deadly gases so successfully that scientists all over the world, particularly the French, considered him to be a butcher. At that time the French were the leading scientists of the world, followed by the Germans and then the British. America had no scientific presence to speak of. It is well-known that when Haber was awarded the Nobel Prize, French Scientists walked out of the award ceremony in Sweden in protest. It was a mass walk out in protest against what they felt was a ceremony honouring a mass-murderer. They were not targeting a national hero. Scientists were pointing their fingers at a fellow-scientist. It must be remembered that after the war scientists emerged from their wartime research to speak out against war. However, the contribution of these scientists in the earlier part of their careers must not be forgotten, for humans find themselves through their past experiences.

In science or in any other field, the insights obtained early in one's career cannot be ignored in later life, so it must be remembered that scientists who spoke out against war later were once, out of patriotism or any other reason, involved in military research. But their perceptions remained sharp. An example of this is the distinguished scientist Peter Kapitza who was awarded the Nobel Prize nearly forty years after his work on electromagnetic fields and cryogenics along with two other scientists for their totally unrelated work on cosmic rays and particle physics. When he rose to receive his prize for work he had done nearly half a century ago, Kapitza did not speak about the research which had earned him his award, as was the custom. Instead he remarked that since his findings were quite old, he would talk about the work his children were engaged in instead, and chose to slight the Nobel Committee's acknowledgement in this brilliant fashion. Anyway the way Kapitza, the Nobel laureate of 1978, distinguished between atom bombs and atomic energy is fascinating: 'To speak about atomic energy in terms of the atom bomb is comparable with speaking about electricity in terms electric chair.' Need there be further explanation? No one believes that our world can run without electricity, yet the reaction the word electricity produces has nothing in common with the thrill of horror the words 'electric chair' produces. There is the same gulf between the words 'atom bomb' and 'atomic energy'. Scientists like Kapitza, or the French scientist and president of the Atomic Power Commission, Frederic Juliet Curie who announced publicly at a press conference that although he and his colleagues would do further research on atomic energy, it would be used for peaceful purposes only, or any of the other scientists mentioned above never fought in any war themselves. Most of them wished atomic energy to be used for the betterment of human life. This is a cruel joke. One may create a missile, someone else an anti-missile, yet another person an anti-anti-missile. The same process may go on with ever more powerful atom bombs being created by different people who might be said to be enemies, but the inventors of these weapons, or others used on the battlefield, like rifles or guns never fight on the field with them. Yet they are the ones who appeal to the conscience of the common man or to the heads of governments to stop war. This point will help us understand where the real strength of the peace movement lies. It is commonly believed that peace protests are ineffective, but history tells us otherwise. Any discussion touching war and peace must include Albert Einstein. His *Ideas and Opinions* expresses many anti-war sentiments. At the time of the Los Alamos Project, Einstein was persuaded of his popularity with the American public, and that with his support the project would be able to create the bomb. The man who persuaded him was a Hungarian scientist called Leo Szilard who had been driven out of his native country by Hitler. It was after this that the bomb was created. The names of those who helped create it must be noted, nearly every important scientist from Feynman, to Neils Bohr, to Oppenheimer, Otto Hahn, Straussman and Lise Meitner were involved. But it was the U.S. Military which was in charge of the project. Robert Junk's *Brighter than Thousand Suns* records the role General Grover played there. The world had never before witnessed such a gathering of scientific genius as that which occurred at Los Alamos, but it was the U.S. Army which controlled the project once Einstein convinced the U.S. President to create the bomb. After Hiroshima-Nagasaki, Einstein suffered a nervous breakdown for several weeks, muttering and tearing his hair out while asking himself why he had discovered the formula $E = mc^2$ (the formula is the key to creating the atom bomb). Laura Fermi, the wife of Enrico Fermi, the Italian physicist writes of how her husband tried to flatter the Italian dictator Mussolini by proposing to name an element he had discovered after him. He had hoped that the Mussolini might spare him for although Fermi was not Jewish himself, his wife Laura was. However, like Franco, Hitler and other similar people, Mussolini was no fool, and he replied that he had heard that the new element was radioactive, and emitted rays/particles to change into a new element, and added 'I am not that much unstable, I am not that much unstable'. Frightened, Fermi soon fled. Another instance is that of Linus Pauling, the 'wonder of the twentieth century' who won the Nobel Prize twice, one of only four people to do so. When Linus Pauling won the Peace Prize for campaigning against atomic/nuclear war, one of the most popular magazines of America, *Life*, published interviews with several leading scientific experts of America. One of them was Edward Taylor, who dreamed of building an atom bomb, built new bombs and wrote nursery rhymes for children, such as 'A for atom, B for bomb'. The reason seems to be that children needed to be taught things like this, and not about like flowers and birds, to raise them to be butchers. Anyway one of the scientists interviewed pointed out that awarding a second Nobel to Linus Pauling was even more insulting to the United States of America than a slap on the face of its President. The journal of the American Chemical

Society published an article vilifying the same Linus Pauling. The editors refused to let him publish a defence. Pauling resigned from the society.

The president of the women's peace movement worldwide was Nobel laureate Irene Curie. When the American scientists' association proposed to present her with an honorary fellowship, the politics behind the scenes was such that American scientists protested that Irene Curie was a danger to security because of her association with peace movements. This was an embarrassment for both the American scientific community and Irene Curie. In 1954, Linus Pauling's book *No More War* demonstrates how someone in a responsible position can speak out against war. Two more scientists are worth mentioning in this regard. One is a Hungarian scientist Albert von Szent-Gyorgi, who wrote a book, *The Crazy Ape* in 1970, when the US was conducting its twisted war against Vietnam. Szent-Gyorgi was awarded the Nobel Prize for discovering Vitamin C. He shot himself in the arm to avoid the battlefield. He expressed his views on war: 'Wars, bloodshed and destruction the representatives of these forces bring kings, barons, dictators, generals and the like.... Most wars were not decided by the glorious kings or heroic generals but by rats and lice.' His reasoning was that it was the rats and lice 'which carried infections and spread plagues'. Nor would anyone believe that a Nobel laureate could possibly express the following sentiments: 'The height of the pedestals of the statues we erect to our national heroes is mostly proportional to the number of peoples they killed as Bertrand Russell remarked: To my mind the real heroes of mankind are the Galileos, Newtons, Darwins, Pasteurs, Shakespeares, etc., etc.' This may serve to reassure us that there is still hope for this world. Science and technology may have been used to create more advanced deadly weapons but the foremost scientists of the world have always raised their voices in protest. Jorgi has also given a fascinating account of how a warmongering U.S. government views statistics. He sums up the American philosophy of war in one remarkable line, 'one death is a tragedy, one lakh deaths are statistics'. This line is worth remembering in the context of Hiroshima-Nagasaki, and other such episodes. Research for the atom bomb and Hiroshima and Nagasaki are two things which repeatedly crop up in this discussion on science and human progress, but it must be remembered that almost each and every scientist—except Edward Taylor—has clearly spoken out against war. After witnessing the atom bomb explode, Leo Szilard, who had persuaded Einstein to join him, stood up and vowed that he would never again conduct any research in physics and that he would henceforth restrict himself to the life sciences. Szilard kept his vow. Otto Hahn who had won the Nobel for his work on atomic fission, attempted suicide on more than one occasion. He would frequently wake up at night, haunted by the thought that it was his research which had enabled the massacre of Hiroshima and Nagasaki. When Lise Meitner fled through Holland and Denmark to Sweden, the Swedish king offered her as much money as she could want to work on creating an atom bomb. The king had extended his protection to her from Hitler, and given her shelter in his country, and Lise Meitner expressed her awareness of this and her gratitude for it. But she pleaded that she could not do what he asked for she had resolved never to work on creating an atom bomb. When Albert Einstein was offered the post of President of Israel he declined. Szent-Gyorgi too was offered the post of the President of Hungary and he too declined. These facts are important when we consider that the President responsible for organizing the research which created the atom bomb, did not reject the presidential post. The scientists who conducted the atomic research which created the bomb, however, did not associate themselves with any government. The duty of the common people then is clear. It is not to try and outdo Ronald Reagan's Star Wars weaponry by creating weapons many times more powerful. It lies in joining the path walked by Albert Einstein, by Linus Pauling, by Szent-Gyorgi, by Lise Meitner, by Otto Hahn, by Zilard and Straussman and strengthening the campaign for peace. The establishment of the World Trade Organization has changed the face of war. How it has done so may be discussed on another occasion. What is relevant here is that the conscience of the entire world must be aroused and organized in order present an ordered front against all forms of insanity. The World Social Forum in Mumbai saw people of all beliefs and religions joining forces; something similar must be organized and in fact, there are signs of such a movement worldwide. It is disheartening to think of how a dedicated leader and Nobel laureate like Yasser Arafat was placed under house arrest with the threat of violence while the world of the twenty-first century watched in silence. There are no great personalities in the world now, there is no Einstein or Bertrand Russell, no Maxim Gorky, no Rabindranath Tagore or Picasso any more. That role must be taken up and their legacy must be fulfilled by us. Only then can we build the world of our dreams.

# The Ways of Dying in Retrospect: A Study on Care for and Rights to Live

11

*Suman Nath, Gopalkrishna Chakraborti* and
*Priyadarsini Sengupta*

While exploring the existentially perceptual 'being' of terminally ill cancer patients from phenomenological perspective, different schemas of human existence are brought into being. The study incorporates field interactions at one suburban cancer hospital near Kolkata and qualitative Internet chat research especially with people from USA, Germany and France. These two broad contexts of experiences project different voices of multidimensional living with terminal illness. The differences in the themes reflect their mode of perceiving the Self, World and 'Other' in the world of numbered days.

The perspectives spanning from positivism to participatory approaches encourage the present authors to select qualitative approach in general and phenomenology in particular allowing a closer acquaintance with the phenomenon of interest. The data were collected in the form of *situated description* by means of the process of painstaking participation and emotional discourses close to what we may call empathy. Analysing the co-constructed interactions showed the differences in the modes of being terminally ill in different contexts. These differences are actually determining the way people die with economic and mental [dis]order and the way people live with aided 'opportunity' in last few days at hospital. These schemas as an outcome of the contexts of experience project the serious human rights issues in broader sense of health care discourses and positive attitude to the life as such.

## Introduction: The Great Evidential Differences

> I lost a lot.... The assurances of a long future, seeing my children marry and have children. I had been going to college to further my education in nursing. Now with permanent short-term memory loss I've lost my career. With having post-thoracotomy syndrome I have a lot of pain every day doing menial jobs at home. But I have also been very blessed because I am still alive today. I thank the Lord and my Doctors for that.
>
> —*Evelin, a thirty-two-year old woman (USA)*

> All my friends of school and college are happily leading their life. They have their own families, children, and I am here in this hospital dying everyday.
>
> —*Revari, a thirty-five-year old woman (India)*

> You have to be positive and expect success. Never give up hope. Live life to the fullest and don't let cancer hold you back from doing anything and everything you want. Check

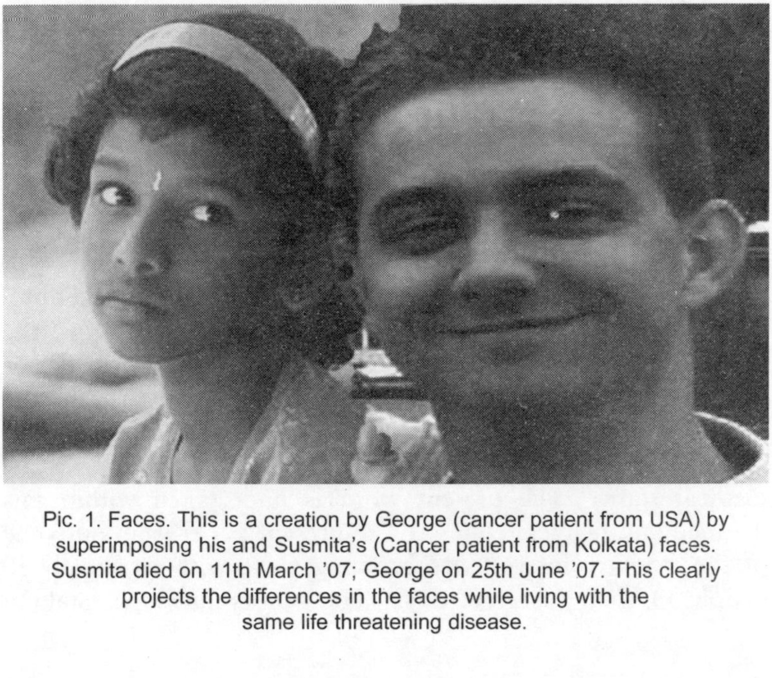

Pic. 1. Faces. This is a creation by George (cancer patient from USA) by superimposing his and Susmita's (Cancer patient from Kolkata) faces. Susmita died on 11th March '07; George on 25th June '07. This clearly projects the differences in the faces while living with the same life threatening disease.

up after check up I continue to be cancer free. I learned it throughout my life.

*—Jen, a forty-seven-year-old man (Germany)*

I always thought that I was strong and then in the middle of the night I used to cry, sitting beside the window, when it was full moon. There was complete silence. The moon had an amazing effect on the water of the Ichhamati.[1] I used to cry for something I never knew.

*—Shankar, a fifty-year-old man (India)*

I became very close with my doctors, the hospital staff and other patients. Their friendship played a very important role in my childhood and in helping my parents cope with me being sick. The best part of my past is my future and that I can help make others aware of Wilms tumors. As a teenager I befriended with a girl at school who was so interested in what I had gone through that she did a report on Wilms tumors. We are still best friends today!

*—Pouro, an eighteen-year-old girl (France)*

Can you tell me why my mother hates me, why she ignores my existence! Can't I survive? Believe me I want to live!

*—Paromita, a nineteen-year-old girl (India)*

Health as a fundamental human right was recognized in the World Health Organization's Constitution stating that the enjoyment of the highest attainable standard of health is one of the fundamental rights of every human being without distinction of race, religion, and political belief, economic or social condition.[2] Patient's rights largely confine themselves to regulating the relationship between the patient and the health care provider or institution (Bijl, 2000). However, in the area of health, the individual is very much dependent on good advice because the expertise, skills and knowledge are in the hands of others, i.e. the medical staffs.[3] The present work is undertaken within this dreaded and helpless context. The present paper is an outcome of the primary interest of becoming close with terminally ill people in their last few days. The self-assigned painstaking endeavour is undertaken to see what changes in emotions, beliefs and attitudes towards self, life, and world took place during and after being aware of terminal illness. And, why? There are two broad contexts of interactions involved. The first is the direct interactions within a suburban hospital near Kolkata. The second is an outcome of qualitative chat research with cancer patients from USA, Germany and France. These three countries are taken within a single paradigm owing to logic that all representatives from these countries are treated at free of cost. Apart from the free treatment they also enjoy certain other aids like good hospital association and free interactions with other people via World Wide Web. The suburban cancer hospital near Kolkata on the other hand represents the economic problems with the cost of the treatment and also the problem of proper communication.

The data are analysed primarily by empirical phenomenological method to find out schemas of terminal human existence. The phenomenological schemas in turn showed a sharp difference in the ways of continuing the last few days under treatment. Though the primary interest was not to find out the differences but with the fieldwork it revealed afterwards.

In the present paper we project firstly the patients' experiences from subjective perspective with an aim to grasp the mental directedness. Secondly, an endeavour is made to find out the differences in the ways of dying with the help of phenomenological schemas. Thirdly, an attempt is made to find out the reason of these differences and finally an emphasis on the importance to use the qualitative and inductive methodology for addressing the sensitive issues like terminal illness. The critical methodological clarification is of central importance in order to address the issues and have a proper understanding of what rights are, how rights are projected even in silent way of dying and what importance rights hold in the context care giving.

## Rights: The Way We See

The concept of human rights in United Nations' voice is considered as universal an inalienable.[4] However, with our present postmodern perception of local and fragmented reality (Lyotard,

1984) and our consciousness of postcolonial arguments it is logical not to treat human rights as universal. Rather human rights in its present universal voice project just another 'western' creation. For us it is based on European tradition where individuals are separable from their society. We like questioning whether these rights can apply to collectivist and communitarian societies that view the individual as indivisible element of the whole society. Substantively their value judgement ought to be not our value judgement. There can never be a universal standard that can be used to judge any society. Though we know these arguments can be conquered by the rhetorical benefit of human rights that they are so fundamental, so basic to human existence that they should trump over any other considerations. We agree with this contention too, but we like to incorporate the voice of the people about whom rights are projected.

However, for the present paper we rather adopt a substantive formulation of O'Manique (1990). We feel that human rights should be founded upon something inherent to humans rather than some moral vision that is created by human action. We adopt here O'Manique's propositions that:

P.1 I ought to survive.

P.2 'X' is necessary for my survival.

P.3 Therefore I ought to do/have 'X'.

These contentions are also not out of hurdle. The first problem comes from within the first proposition. Many societies value sacrifice but these are usually for the sake of the survival of the others. However, in the present context we firmly assert the survival is of prime importance. With present condition of the terminal illness we rather put our bias for the positive living of those people who are living with life threatening emergency.

## Methodology: Journey to the Need Perception

With our agreement with O'Manique (1990) it becomes important to find out the 'X'. The 'X' may not be always prominent especially in a delicate field like terminal illness. Most often people we encountered were either physically too weak to talk or were too depressed with no mood of continuing discussions of any sort. Our understanding was to apply personal information as a source of knowledge: their 'interpretation' in practice to get to the things themselves. The present concern was largely non-intervening and hardly had any set or patterned questions in a sense inductive logic were appropriate.

## Approaches

The literature related to the study of dying showed clearly identifiable phases of development. The first was heavily influenced by the positivism. It identified dying in terms of medicalisation and bureaucratisation (Blauner, 1966; Charmaz, 1980; Cassell, 1974; Shorter, 1986; De Zeeuw, 1993). While rephrasing with Foucault (1972) it is the scientific attitude where dying became meaningless activity. The second self-termed care discourse with Kubler-Ross (1969) put on importance on the subjective, social and mental dimension (Dubois, 1980) associated with dying. However, with the phase-wise division of dying in reified sense hindered the process of subjectification. The third was the research with participative approach where dying patients; their family members, friends and caregivers co-operated each other for developing collective strategies for shifting from 'care for dying' to 'care for living' (Krouwel, 1991). The ultimate aim was to find out a more humane way of living in those last few days (Lukken, 1984). Though these approaches were fruitful for gathering and projecting information but provided us little guidance to project our intended subjective experience without intervening or creating disturbance to their life. Participatory actor approach was catchy and noble but we hardly had a chance to convince the potential participants.

## Why Phenomenology?

Within this messy situation we started doing fieldwork without the aid of any clear idea or patterned questions. We used to write as much as we could soon after we returned from the field. While doing qualitative chatting we used to save a version of the chat text. While thinking about the concept formation we started thinking about doing some sort of *INDUCTION*. We learned the particularly serving logic of induction from grounded theory (Glaser and Strauss, 1967;

Chenitz and Swanson, 1986). However, for being closer to the sense data grounded theory was not enough. The sense data was a source of problem, as it was required to provide insights into the radicalness in respondent's inward affective situational and contextual states through sharing experiences that were often very personal. Phenomenology was thought to be serving best owing to the fact that it starts with the data itself and then helps finding the schemas of human existence (Polkinghorne, 1982). More importantly our aim to identify consistent conscious and unconscious mental activity that could be converted into useful information was quite satisfactorily fulfilled.

## Phenomenology: The Way We Did

With Husserlian (1931, 1989) descriptive approach we became aware that we were to involve in a continuous cycle of perception and reflection on the experience to grasp 'its essence'. The concept of lifeworld (Husserl [1913b] 1989: 411) with its continuous existence within the literature with Alfred Schütz (1975, 1976) further shaped our perceptions. However, for doing aspect of phenomenology in the present situation some contemporary publications like Clark Moustakas (1994) and Robert Schweitzer (2002) helped us to involve in doing empirical phenomenology. Amedeo Giorgi in a series of publications (Giorgi, 1975, 1985, 1992a, 1992b, 1994) shaped our idea about doing interpretative phenomenological enquiry by gaining a sense of the whole transcript. With this sense we made the discrimination of meaning units to find out the Natural Meaning Unit (NMU) ultimately leading to a synthesis of transformed meaning. However, for gaining the NMU we did a four steps transcript analysis:

1. **Describing thick** in a manner that incorporated expressions words and also minute detailing of different expressions, tone of voice, pause.
2. **Coding** to find out different themes and sub-themes.
3. **Lumping** these themes and sub-themes to map out the stable aspect of the experience: a step towards abstraction.

4. **Comparing** these themes in said two broad contexts to find out the voice of the 'things themselves'.

However, for the present purpose of voice projection in terms of depicting the mental directedness and relating the whole scenario with fundamental rights it is not necessary to present the details of the four stages. Rather we are presenting the themes in a comparative way which is an outcome of all these four steps.

## Themes: Ways of Dying/Living

### *Pain*

Pain as a dimension of terminal illness showed different aspects related to both the physical and existential mental pain.

In the hospital interaction 'pain' came up as a dimension related to the way of living. There is a dimension of suppression. This is very much evident in the case of the younger people interacted with. They have either suffered or been suffering for very long periods of time, or are feeling being alienated from their family life. As their disease progressed they started feeling being left alone. This is very much related with the decreased amount of familial and peer care compared to what they used to get before falling ill. They tried to suppress their physical pain because they did not want to bother 'others'. There is a sharp variation in discourses concerning pain. There are instances where the nature of discourses concerning pain differs even among patients suffering from the same cancer types. This variation shows a sharp contrast in terms of age. While older people provided a detailed description of pain, younger people did not care to do so. As the disease progressed many aged people continued their descriptions tirelessly. The monotony of the themes about their pain and suffering never stopped them from continuing such detailed discourses.

In sum in the hospital interaction there are:

P.1 Dimensions of suppression.

P.2 Variations among discourses in terms of age.

P.3 Mental and bodily pain having a cumulative effect on living.

In the case of online interactions the discourses concerning the physical pain are almost exclusively absent. Probed with straightforward questions about their bodily pain, they used to reply in the past tense. Their physical pain, however painful, decreased after receiving treatment. They would rather describe how they got rid of the pain than the pain itself. They are aware about what type of treatment they are going to get and what medicines gave them relief. This knowledge of treatment along with constant interactions gave them the relief from both their physical and mental pain. This is a part of their overall positive attitude towards life rather than being oriented towards death. In addition, they have displayed less evidence of suffering from mental pain. There is no instance of suppression of feelings. There are instances where the participatory approach has helped reduce the mental pain. The hospital interaction between patients, their family members and friends have eased their way a lot. Their care for living rather than care for dying helps stop creating the creation of an image of mental pain.

Summarily, these are:

P.1 Total/Complete absence of physical pain.

P.2 Technical minimization of mental pain, thus decreasing concern.

P.3 Life-orientedness, rather than death-orientedness.

***Fear***

Fear in its present sense agrees with Rachman's (1990) formulation of feeling of apprehension about tangible and predominantly realistic dangers to relate to collective human and expressions of sensing threat, fear and/or anxiety.

In the hospital interactions fear is found to develop in association with the bodily pain. As the pain increases the fear becomes related to a belief of being pushed close to death. The context of being admitted in a cancer hospital is another cause of fear. A common feeling about being admitted to a cancer hospital is the incurability of the disease and the painful nature of the resulting death. Probing with carefully selected questions invariably revealed that at its core, fear is always associated with death. And with this fear of death, other dimensions of fear are often associated. Young adults often fear leaving their business unfinished. Married men worry about the fate of their family after they are dead. Older people, on the other hand, are more afraid of the remnant of their painful existence than the death itself.

In sum the fear shows:

F.1 Rooted from and resulting in cumulative factors of pain.

F.2 Context of being treated in the 'Cancer hospital' another dimension of fear.

F.3 Fear of loss, unfinished business.

F.4 Fear of living with pain of cancer rather than death.

Online interaction shows a much different scenario. In this case too, fear starts with bodily pain. With admission to the hospital there is a continuous decrease in fear. The sheer pain that they used to experience before being admitted to the hospital is relieved. They can, however, sometimes remember the pain in their dreams. Jeniffer, a thirty-year-old woman with brain cancer reported the return of the pain in her dream. In the dream, it was as painful as in real life, and so she refused sleeping pills to avoid dreaming as far as possible. The fear of the return of the pain is evidenced.

At the hospital, they felt the pain of isolation from their 'normal' life. The more they stayed at the hospital the more they felt a good 'social' environment from something called hospital association. Patients who had spent some months or years with the hospital association have reported a pain of leaving the association when they were declared cured. Many of them are still in touch with the association. They encourage others by sharing their stories of survival, restoring the fact that cancer is not equal to death.

In sum 'fear' from the chat room interaction shows:

F.1 It starts from the bodily discomfort.

F.2 There is a fear of return of pain.

F.3 Having dreadful dreams is also a source of fear.

### *Isolation*

Isolation in its present usage represents a feeling and not any physical separation. Since with hospitalisation a separation from the regular activities was unavoidable, how the separation have engrossed the mental directedness is the concern.

Isolation in hospital interactions is found to be associated with increasing detachment from active normal life. As a process, it starts even before detection. Physical weakness and increasing separation from regular life enhances the feeling of being isolated. As the disease progresses hospitalisation takes place with complete exclusion from the rest of the world, which compels people to express their antipathy to their existential situation. These expressions in turn creates problem of adjustment for family members living with a crisis.

Hospital world creates relational complexities. People find Monotony in the hospital with patterned discourses of physical condition and medical inputs. Irritation, lack of patience and misbehaviour as a consequence becomes a frequent phenomenon. Limited queries about medication and health condition enhance further the feeling of isolation from the rest of the world. Mansur, a forty-year-old patient suffering from lung cancer narrated his story of increasing maladjustment with his wife.

> I still love my wife. I know she misses me very much. She is tensed, agonised. I can understand that. But how could I tolerate this monotonous situation. It is like we are living only in a world of medicine. I cannot find me belonging within her. She is treating me like a 'thing', a diseased body…now I feel that throughout my life I was living only to support…no one ever understood me. I was just a machine for earning…when this machine stopped earning the sole concern is about the future after my death. No one, not even my wife bothers about what I feel, what I need. Day after day she kept asking me how I am feeling. Did I take medicines in time or not, what would happen to her after my death?...

Summarily, isolation in hospital interaction shows these following dimensions:

I.1 It starts with detachment from regular life.

I.2 As a consequence of hospitalisation exclusion from family and work place becomes inevitable. This exclusion enhances the feeling being isolated.

I.3 Monotony in discourses and life in the hospital adds negative dimension to the feeling isolation.

In chat room interaction, the isolation is found to develop with the detachment from the 'normal' life. Initial bodily pain and exclusion from the workplace enhance the feeling of being excluded but there are factors stop increasing this feeling. These factors start acting with hospitalization. Medication eliminates bodily pain, which gives them confidence to continue. At hospital, they also encounter something called 'hospital association'. Through hospital association, they interact with other cancer patients, which confiscate loneliness. This communication and interaction through sharing of experiences minimise the fear of 'unknown'. Positive effect in socio-medical terms is that their participation to healing process increases even further. Their continuous knowledge sharing with co-patients, their family members and caregivers enhances their interests in the treatment process. Michael a forty-seven-years-old man from Bordeaux of France reports:

> Week after week with treatment I became cancer free. The initial fear was gone for ever. My friends at hospital, my family members and docs managed the situation well. It wasn't too much later that they thought my cancer had come back. Come to find out that I was given a lot of Radiation which had caused bone loss to my arm. I then had to have a bone graft. I had 2 plates put in and tons of screws. And you know it was a very interesting experience for me.

However, it would be an overstatement to say that they do not feel isolated. They admit this fact too. Catherine a twenty-seven-year-old woman from Denver shared her experience of this feeling:

> I know in my battles, I've always felt a bit isolated, as when I was younger, I was one of the youngest cancer

> cases around. So, I never really knew anyone I could directly relate to in an aspect of what I was dealing with, between the loss of my leg (which never slowed me much anyhow), or just in knowing someone who also went through something similar around that age. At times with my more recent battles, I've thought it would be cool to connect with other 20-somethings as well who are either fighting cancer or are past their battles, as there's not so many of us dealing with cancer by this age. I had a difficult time dealing with this at times, as pretty much anyone would, but I've stayed positive and focused on beating the challenges as they came. I'm looking to network with other 20-somethings to chat and share mutual support...always good to rally up the troops!

Making network and sharing of experiences is the key factor to cope with and transform the situation of isolation.

In sum isolation as experienced by chat room people includes:

- I.1 An initial feeling of detachment from regular life.
- I.2 Increasing attachment with the hospital association, knowledge and experience sharing, minimization of fear of the unknown.
- I.3 The feeling of isolation continues but it does not act as a determining factor in those last days.

### *Loneliness*

Loneliness is experienced in association with the initial isolation. It is mostly an after-effect of isolation from regular activities and hospitalization.

In hospital interaction, there are instances where people became victim of loneliness even before being admitted in the hospital. While probing deeper loneliness is found to develop with isolation from 'normal' living and as frustration from the continuous suffering and ineffective treatment.

At initial stages, the loneliness becomes an outcome of the discovery of something 'different'. Ahedur a thirty-three-year-old man reports that he felt alone when he used to wake up in the middle of the night, watching 'others' sleeping. This feeling

Pic. 2 Sketch of Promila made by Mr. Goutam Bakshi —an artist from Kolkata.[5]

of having something different compelled Promila to become introverted. Her silence used to 'speak' thousand words that her mother reported she failed to understand. Later conversation reveals the fact that she started loving the loneliness. In her last few days we found her talking even lesser. The complete emersion in the loneliness acted fanatically. With the loss of activities, mental distortion, and complete living with loneliness speeds up the process of dying as the medicines stop affecting the way it is expected.

Loneliness with hospital interaction shows:

L.1 A feeling of having something different is the cause of the loneliness.

L.2 With time, a complete emersion to the loneliness is reported.

In chat room interactions, loneliness is a past theme. As found in the hospital interaction, chat room people also reported that they faced loneliness after being aware of their serious illness. This is partially because of their awareness of the dreaded future, and physical pain that they found none can share. The isolation from regular activities created and enhanced the image of being lonely. With the hospitalization it decreases. The hospital gives an isolated yet attractive way of living. This new life at the hospital gives them the spirit to fight without the pain of their battleship.

Loneliness in chat room interaction reflects:

> Something past that started with the disease and alienation from the regular life but minimised with the hospitalization.

## Nostalgia

Sharing memories repeatedly is one of the important aspects of the present experience. With this aspect the other dimensions like loneliness, isolation are prominently reflected.

In the hospital interaction, sharing of memories is frequent. With their continuity at the hospital the isolation starts acting upon them. There are different dimensions interacted. Wishful affection with friends, loved ones, family members, bedroom, strange places, work place, and dreams all have came alive with different narrations. These nostalgic memories are wonderful in the sense of our anthropological and humanitarian quest. All these reflect the degree of our attachments with people interacted. Sharing of these memories soon revealed the negative aspect. The negative aspect is their living with memories. Tireless narrations and repetition of the same story for several times compel us to feel that they had started living in to an unreal world. Their switching over to the past and ignorance to the present makes it difficult to treat them. They denied their situation of living with cancer in their last few days. They wanted to live in their unreal simulated world of memories.

Chat room interaction shows their sharing of memories similarly. The nostalgic attachment is present but they show more urge to return to that world without denial of their present situation. They did not have the scope to deny their reality. Rather they loved to be aware of their physical status by being updated with the medicinal inputs. The sharing of experience with other patients and an active participation to the healing process never allows them to deny the reality, which in turn helps the healing process.

## Communication

Differences in the expressions regarding different themes from experiences gathered from both contexts slant us to explore and understand the core. Why these differences arose? Throughout the field interactions, we kept asking this question. With further probing and careful study of different themes, we found the core is the differential communication.

In hospital interaction, the communication is limited and fragmented. Themes of communication with friends and family members are monotonous, centring primarily on the aspect of treatment and bodily comfort. Other dimension of discourses includes the troubles and potential troubles with the economic challenges owing to the treatment cost. With this monotonous communiqué mostly the phase of denial and disgust starts. With denial and disgust, patients stop sharing his/her inner feelings with family members and friends, creating a communication gap. The created image of communication gap afterwards plays objective role. The once created gap enlarges itself taking it to such height that it seems reified and unbreakable.

Chat room people with respect to communication show a sharp contrast. They are enjoying a good hospital association apart from their family and friend circle. Hospital is acting as a medium for finding new friends and developing new relationships. Effective communication persists within the hospital, which also enhances the participation to the healing process. With no exception they are treated free of cost. This cost free treatment in turn not only helps economically but also provides a mental relief. The hospital association with knowledge sharing, sharing of experiences and constant communication between the families of different patients helps creating a positive output. World Wide Web is acting as another medium for them to express, share, and help others to fight the similar situation. Sadly in our chat room interactions we never found a single person from India.

## The Perceived Differences: Projecting Rights

With phenomenological study of our interactions with experiences of terminal illness in two different contexts, a difference in the ways of dying is perceived. With this perception it is now necessary to find out the reason of these differences. With our further induction and probing it is found that at the initial stages of illness the feelings do not vary significantly between people interacted in both the contexts. People from both the contexts report their initial bodily discomfort and pain, fear in association with the discomfort and uncertain future, a feeling of isolation from regular activities and 'normal' (in their consideration) life, loneliness with rapidly changing scenario of their life and nostalgic attachments with past life and activities. However, the differences arose very soon. With our close observations of their dialogues and contexts the differences are clearer. People from chat room reports the complete relief of bodily discomfort—a gift of modern medicalization, though the mentally they feared the return of the pain. With the days without pain they start thinking positively about their painless future. Their initial detachment from their regular life is beautifully supplemented by the hospital association. The positive effect is that the loneliness is a 'thing' from past. They became nostalgic while talking about their past activities, but that too was superficial in a sense they didn't started living with memories.

People interacted at the cancer hospital, on the other hand, continue to suffer from physical pain, and fear of death. Associated with the fear of death is the fear of unfinished business and dreaded economic burden. Even there are instances where they feared living with pain rather than death. The isolation from regular activities, living with dying people, monotonous words concerning their health and a monotonous world compelled them to become lonely. With loneliness many are found to start memorising their past activities. The more dreadful is their living with memories. A complete emersion to the past; living in a simulated environment. Broadly there is a difference in approaching the life with cancer. The difference is between the care for dying and the care for living. While analysing these themes the core is found to be the communication. The sharp difference in the ways of communication as mentioned is making the difference in the ways of dying. It is indeed true if a patient with a certain stage of cancer can only be treated with existing possible medical alternatives. It is also true that the question of survival is not totally depended on the treatment and communication. However, one cannot ignore the impact of difference that we found in our field interactions. People with whom we had interactions in the hospital shared their secrets, innermost feelings with us. Who are we? Are we only anthropologists from a 'remote' world? Or simply a window with which they could share their feelings, ideals, pains and alternative discourses (far from the monotonous queries about their health, well-being and economic hurdles). While chat room people are enjoying their living with hospital association in terms of knowledge sharing, sharing of experiences, and chatting with others via World Wide Web. They are encouraged in *doing for others* in terms of sharing other people's instigated feelings. People interacted in the suburban cancer hospital are, on the other hand, dying with dreaded fear, pain, and pushing their families in an economic crisis.

The effective communication, active living is the magic key that makes all the existential differences. The initial discomforts, mental helplessness, loneliness is conquered by the feeling of belonging with the hospital association at the chat room context. At the Suburban hospital, on the other hand, people are pushed even deeper to these states of minds. It is true that there is an infrastructural difference in the two contexts. However, the rights to live in a more dignified way do not demand much infrastructure. Hospital association, a positive participatory approach in terms of empathic handling of the situation is a need. There is also need of some relaxation in the treatment cost. The way we used emotions and expressions is important. We used to provide them different stories of recovery, a space for alternative topics of discussions like news, sports, movies, our daily activities, jokes, etc. Making them believe that cancer is not much different from other diseases. We acknowledge that ultimately their life depends with medicines but the days they have they should live, not die. They should live their last days not simply continue to die. With participation, interaction this could be achieved. We kept asking what Charmaz (1980) asked in the final chapter that whether social and medical discussions on death and dying really will influence the social organization of death and dying? With Foucault (1972) one could rephrase this, to ask if the care discourse has lead to further structuring (disciplining) of the individual through the significant difference (deviance) of dying. Alternatively can we create or discover possibilities for the de-construction of this ordering and regimentation, which provide the dying with greater control of their own living and dying process? Can we, in other words, have a 'Dying Anarchy' based on the deconstruction of modelled 'dying identities'? Perhaps we can.

Here lies the importance of methodology. It is really hard to approach and project voice from within. The silent ways of dying remained silent until someone starts probing. The qualitative induction, and narrative analysis with phenomenological methodologies as we found can be one of those methods. With comparison and further in-depth analysis one is supposed to find the need (remember that X). Even if those who needed remain silent, dies silently. The data can speak for themselves.

## REFERENCES

Bijl, N. 2000. "Access to Medical Practice and to Medical Acts: Patient Protection and Freedom of Choice", *13th World Congress on Medical Law*. Helsinki, 200-07.

Blauner, R. 1966 "Death and Social Structure." *Psychiatry*, 29 (Nov 1966): 378-94.

Cassell, E. 1974. "Dying in a Technological Society." In Steinfels and Veatch (eds.), *Death Inside Out*. New York: Harper and Row.

Charmaz, C. 1980. *The Social Reality of Death*. Massachusetts: Addison Wesley.

Chenitz, W.C. and Swanson, J.M. 1986. "Qualitative Research using Grounded Theory." In Chenitz, W.C. and Swanson, J.M. (Eds.) *From Practice to Grounded Theory*. pp. 3-15, Menlo Park, CA: Addison-Wesley.

De Zeeuw, G. 1991. "Coordinated Cooperation and Increased Competence." *Knowledge in Society*, 3/4: 114-33.

Dubois, P.M. 1980. *The Hospice Way of Death*. New York: Human Sciences Press.

Foucault, M. 1972. *The Archaeology of Knowledge*. London: Tavistock.

Giorgi, Amedeo. 1975. "An Application of Phenomenological Method in Psychology." In A. Giorgi, C. Fischer and E. Murray (Eds.) *Duquesne Studies in Phenomenological Psychology*, Vol. II, pp. 82-103. Pittsburgh: Duquesne University Press.

—— (Ed.) 1985. *Phenomenology and Psychological Research*, Pittsburgh: Duquesne University Press.

—— 1992a. "Description versus Interpretation: Competing Strategies for Qualitative Research." *Journal of Phenomenological Research*, 23, 119-35.

—— 1992b. "An Exploratory Phenomenological Psychological Approach to the Experience of the Moral Sense." *Journal of Phenomenological Psychology*, 23, 50-86.

—— 1994. "A Phenomenological Perspective on Certain Qualitative Research Methods." *Journal of Phenomenological Psychology*, 25, 190-220.

Glaser, B. and Strauss, A.L. (1967). *The discovery of grounded theory: Strategies for qualitative research*. New York: Adeline.

Husserl, E. 1931. *Ideas toward a pure phenomenology and a phenomenological philosophy*. trans. W.R.B. Gibson. New York: Humanities Press (original work published 1913).

—— [1913b] 1989. *Ideas Pertaining to a Pure Phenomenology and to a Phenomenological Philosophy. Second book: Studies in the Phenomenology of Constitution*, Dordrecht: Kluwer.

Krouwel, M. 1991. *Ik denk ik ben gestorven een papieren dood*. Amsterdam: Thesis publishers.

Kubler-Ross, Elizabeth (1975) *Death: The Final Stage of Growth*. New Jersey: Prentice-Hall, Inc.

Lukken, G. 1984. *Geen leven zonder rituelen*. Baarn: Amboboken.

Lyotard, J.F. 1984. *The Postmodern Condition: A Report on Knowledge*, trans. Ge. Bennington and B. Massumu, Menneapolis: University of Minnesota Press.

Moustakas, C. 1994. *Phenomenological Research Methods*. Thousand Oaks: Sage Publications.

O'Manique, John. 1990. "Universal and Inalienable Human Rights: A Search for Foundations" *Human Rights Quarterly*, pp. 465-85.

Polkinghorne, D. 1982. "What Makes Research Humanistic?" *Journal of Humanistic Psychology*, 22(2), 47-54.

Schütz, Alfred. 1976. *The Phenomenology of the Social World*. London: Heineman Educational Books.

—— 1975. *Collected Papers III: Studies in Phenomenological Philosophy*, The Hague: Nijhoff.

Schweitzer, Robert. 2002. "Editorial." *Indo-Pacific Journal of Phenomenology*, 2(2), 1-2.

Shorter, F. 1986. *Bedside Manners*. New York: Viking, New York.

## NOTES

1. Ichhamati is a river of Bengal.
2. "Promotion of the Rights of Patients in Europe". *WHO*, 1995: 29-44.
3. "European Conference on Health and Human Rights". *Conference Book, Strasbourg* 1999:4.
4. UNIVERSAL DECLARATION OF HUMAN RIGHTS adopted by *General Assembly resolution 217 A (III)* of 10 December 1948. http://www.unhchr.ch/html/menu6/2/fs2.htm
5. Goutam is one of my very close friends. We used to visit Promila together at hospital. Being an artist, Goutam made many sketches of Promila. This one she liked the most. This sketch I feel clearly reflects her melancholia.

# 12

# The Question of Right to Born and to Live: A Study among Rajbansis of a Village in Darjeeling District, West Bengal

*Subir Biswas* and *Ganesh Chandra Mallick*

### Introduction

Gender inequality has many effects on women's lives from birth to death. Women with equal rights are able to seek information about contraceptives and other family planning needs without repercussions from their families or communities. India has a distinctive feature regarding the sex ratio: the century's old deficit of female to male. The sex ratio depends upon some biological factors but various socio-cultural factors also responsible for female deficit. In developing and underdeveloped countries, the problem is more prominent than developed countries. In India, the deficit is largely attributed to women's lower status in society, which has contributed to their higher mortality in all age groups, up to 45 years (Srinivasan, 1994).

The situation is also categorized by the name 'missing females'. Agnihotri by his several studies pointed out causes behind the situation in an Indian scenario (Agnihotri, 1995 and 2000). A lot of studies was conducted in macro level after studied census data and sample surveys, indicating an excess of male child in all age groups as well as prevalence of missing females, because of direct and indirect violence against Indian women (Bhat, 2002; Anuradha et al., 2002; Basudev, 2003; Clark, 1987; Visaria et al., 1981). The factors may be of different types starting from son preference (Clark, 2000; Oldenberg, 1992) to negligence towards female sex (Dasgupta et al., 1998; Jain et al., 1988). The negligence at pregnancy is correlated with maternal mortality (Pal et al., 2002). All the factors resulting high mortality rates of females compared to their male counterpart of all ages (Dyson, 1984; Karkal, 1987; Millar, 1989; Chen, 1982).

The government data in the form of census (Census of India, 2001) or publication from Registrar General of India (Registrar General of India, 1999 and 1992) as well as data from National Family Health Survey (NFHS) indicates greater extent of gender bias resulting female deficit of all age groups (IIPS, 2001).

In India the sex ratio, defined as the number of females per 1000 males (which is opposite to the widely used definition of males per 100 females) has been declining almost consistently over the decades except for a small improvement in the decades 1941-51 (just 1 point), 1971-81 (just 4 point) and 1991-2001 (just 6 points). In West Bengal the sex ratio decline gradually up to 1941, after that it is gradually improved in favour of females. In recent time (2001), it is slightly moderate (just 1 point) than the national level (Table 1) which indicates a comparative trend

**Table 1:** Sex Ratio Pattern of India and West Bengal

| Country/State | 1901 | 1911 | 1921 | 1931 | 1941 | 1951 | 1961 | 1971 | 1981 | 1991 | 2001 |
|---|---|---|---|---|---|---|---|---|---|---|---|
| West Bengal | 945 | 945 | 905 | 890 | 852 | 865 | 878 | 891 | 911 | 917 | 934 |
| India | 972 | 964 | 955 | 950 | 945 | 946 | 941 | 930 | 934 | 927 | 933 |

*Source*: Census of India, 2001.

between India and West Bengal throughout the centuries. The sex ratio of Matigara Block (902) is lower than national level (933). However, the neighbouring blocks of this district possess relatively moderate sex ratio than this block. In case of Darjeeling Phulbazar, Rangli Ranglijot, Kalimpong-I, Kalimpong-II, Gorubathan, Jorebunglo Sukiapokhri, Mirik, Kurseong, Naxalbari, Phansidewa, Kharibari it is 983, 992, 992, 925, 969, 1022, 1001, 982, 911, 950 and 941 respectively (Table 2). The comparative graph of all the blocks is seen on Table 2. We select the village Rangia as a sample, which possess lowest sex ratio within this block (770.92 according to 2001

**Table 2:** Sex Ratio Pattern of Darjeeling Districts (2001)

| No. | Sub-districts | Sex Ratio | | Total |
|---|---|---|---|---|
| | | Rural | Urban | |
| 1. | Darjeeling Phulbazar | 983 | 1026 | 983 |
| 2. | Rangli Ranglijot | 992 | – | 992 |
| 3. | Kalimpong-I | 968 | – | 992 |
| 4. | Kalimpong-II | 925 | – | 925 |
| 5. | Gorubathan | 969 | – | 969 |
| 6. | Jorebunglo Sukiapokhri | 1022 | – | 1022 |
| 7. | Mirik | 1001 | – | 1001 |
| 8. | Kurseong | 982 | 979 | 982 |
| 9. | Matigara | 903 | 876 | 902 |
| 10. | Naxalbari | 911 | 915 | 911 |
| 11. | Phansidewa | 950 | – | 950 |
| 12. | Kharibari | 941 | – | 941 |
| | Darjeeling | 956 | 917 | 943 |

*Source*: Census of India, 2001.

census) and the present work done among Rajbansi population of this village which has a maximum share of total village population. Both biological and bio-social factors responsible for female deficit such as sex ratio at birth, fertility rate of the population, sex specific mortality rate (infant mortality and mortality as a whole), disease treatment pattern, age at marriage, age at first birth, literacy rate, child preference, etc. (Oldenberg, 1992; Krisnaji, 1987; Sundri et al., 1994). The aim of the paper is to examine how the above said factors influence sex ratio among Rajbansi population of village Rangia, of district Darjeeling in West Bengal, India.

## Materials and Methods

An anthropological study was conducted during 11 January 2004 to 26 June 2004 in Rangia village of Matigara block, Darjeeling district, West Bengal. The village Rangia was chosen because of its peculiarity in this field, as it has lowest sex ratio in the Matigara block; again Matigara block exhibit lowest sex ratio of district Darjeeling. The Rajbansi community was selected because of its strength on this village. About 976 Rajbansi people of 200 families was studied, among them 525 are males and 451 are females of various age groups. The selection of Rajbansi population of said village is near about 100% except 10-15 families.

A census scheduled was prepared for this study and was filled in directly from the field. Beside census schedule, observation and interviews was done. Secondary data was collected from census reports, sample surveys, books and journals.

For statistical inference simple percentage and average calculation was done. Beside this, the study also calculates sex ratio of various ages and various groups. In demography, as per international definition, the sex ratio may be defined as the number of males per thousand females in a population. In India, in contrary, the sex ratio is defined as the number of females per thousand males. As the present study sometimes compare the field data with Indian census, the second definition was used to calculate the sex ratio of the population. To calculate the Sex Ratio of the population as well as of different categories of the population, the following calculation was conducted using standard formula (Srinivasan, 1998). The sex ratio of this study was obtained by using following formula Sex Ratio = (Number of females in a population at a specific time / Number of males in the population at that specific time) × 1000.

## Results and Discussion

The age-sex structure of the village shows slightly different characteristics feature than ideal. More or less males are dominated in all age groups (Table 3). The age-sex structure or population pyramid (Table 3) shows an imbalance between male and female, favouring males, of all age groups except 20-24, 30-34, and 35-39, which shows a reverse picture of high female representation. The study suggests that the reverse situation of 20-24, 30-34 and 35-39 is due to immigration of females mostly due to marriage. However, remaining age groups exhibit a declining sex ratio, due to lower female participation in all age groups. The above said three exceptions also resulting from more male participation as more number of female in-migration to the village than their out-migrant counterpart because of marriage.

**Table 3:** Age-Sex Structure of the Population

| Age group | Male | Female | | Total | Sex Ratio |
|---|---|---|---|---|---|
| | | No. | % | | |
| 0 – 4 | 56 | 49 | 105 | 10.76 | 875 |
| 5 – 9 | 57 | 50 | 107 | 10.96 | 877.19 |
| 10 – 14 | 69 | 46 | 115 | 11.78 | 666.67 |
| 15 – 19 | 55 | 49 | 104 | 10.65 | 890.91 |
| 20 – 24 | 43 | 60 | 103 | 10.55 | 1395.35 |
| 25 – 29 | 56 | 45 | 101 | 10.35 | 803.57 |
| 30 – 34 | 38 | 46 | 84 | 8.61 | 1210.53 |
| 35 – 39 | 32 | 39 | 71 | 7.27 | 1218.75 |
| 40 – 44 | 34 | 12 | 46 | 4.71 | 352.94 |
| 45 – 49 | 31 | 26 | 57 | 5.84 | 838.71 |
| 50 – 54 | 25 | 18 | 43 | 4.41 | 720 |
| 55 – 59 | 12 | 4 | 16 | 1.64 | 333.33 |
| 60 – 64 | 8 | 3 | 11 | 1.13 | 375 |
| 65 – 69 | 5 | 2 | 7 | 0.72 | 400 |
| 70 + | 4 | 2 | 6 | 0.62 | 500 |
| Total | 525 | 451 | 976 | 100 | 859.05 |

*Source*: Present Field Work, 2004.

The sex ratio at birth is one of the 'initial conditions', which determines the sex ratio of overall population. It is nearly constant within a range of 104-07 males' live birth per 100 females live birth (i.e. sex ratio varies from 934.57-961.53) in absence of any sex selective human intervention (Mc. Kee, 1984). According to National Family Health Survey Report, (1992-93) sex ratio at birth in India was 938.08 and in West Bengal, it was around 938.08-940.73. Among Rajbansi population of the village the sex ratio at birth is much more lower (843.9) than country level

**Table 4:** Sex ratio at Birth in India, West Bengal and Rangia Village

| Region | Sex Ratio at Birth |
|---|---|
| India* | 938.08 |
| West Bengal* | 938.08-940.73 |
| Rangia# | 843.9 |

*Source: *NFHS, 1992-93*; # Present field work, 2004.

or state level (Table 4). Table 4 shows the comparative situation of Rangia with India and West Bengal. The lower sex ratio at birth may be one of the root causes of declining sex ratio of later stages. In addition, it may arise the question of right to born, as the field experience indicates a sex selective abortion, though the process of identification of foetus sex is not scientific. It is mostly depend on *ojhas* (traditional medical practitioner) magico-religious practices. The field data identified 13 such abortions, among them 11 were girls and remaining 2 boys.

The fertility rate of the population and the sex ratio changes over a period in India (Sundri, 1994) as well as in West Bengal. Now the fertility rate has decline from the past, because of acceptance of family planning programme. The sex ratio scenario indicates the deliberate choice by parents among the number of females to the 'total neglect of the female children' (Miller, 1989). The adoption of standard family planning methods once an 'ideal family' (skewed in favour of sons) has been reached with this ideal family, a family planning strategy that says, 'stop having children after two sons have been born and reject up to death fourth born daughter' (Oldenburg, 1992). This scenario is very much similar among the Rajbansi population of Rangia village; Table 5 projects the population according to the desire of children as well as the sex ratio of different types of family. Whereas Table 6 projects child preference of the spouses based on their educational status as well as sex ratio for each groups. It is obvious that education accelerate consciousness, which may be utilized positively or negatively.

Table 5 also suggests a positive correlation of sex ratio with family size, i.e. in case of small sized family, the sex ratio is relatively lower than that of larger sized family. The reason may be multifold, but it may be argued that small family size disturbs equilibrium by way of selections not to have any children after one. Again, Table 6 indicates that child preferences may be correlated with educational level of father and mother. As the educational level of father or mother increases, the proportion of girl child is also increases. The educational status of mother may

**Table 5:** Family Size based on Sex Ratio and Child Preference

| No. of Family | 1st Child | 2nd Child | 3rd Child | 4th Child | 5th Child | Male | Female | Total | Sex Ratio | Son preference | Daughter preference |
|---|---|---|---|---|---|---|---|---|---|---|---|
| 7 | D | - | - | - | - | 7 | 14 | 21 | 2000 | 2 (28.57) | 3 (42.86) |
| 15 | S | - | - | - | - | 30 | 15 | 45 | 500 | 8 (53.33) | 2 (13.33) |
| **Total-22** | - | - | - | - | - | **37** | **29** | **66** | **783.78** | **10 (45.45)** | **5 (22.73)** |
| 43 | S | S | - | - | - | 129 | 52 | 182 | 403.1 | 27 (62.79) | 3 (6.98) |
| 40 | D | S | - | - | - | 80 | 81 | 161 | 1012.5 | 23 (57.5) | 4 (10.00) |
| 13 | S | D | S | - | - | 39 | 31 | 70 | 794.87 | 8 (61.54) | 1 (7.69) |
| 23 | D | D | S | - | - | 46 | 69 | 115 | 1500 | 15 (65.22) | 2 (8.70) |
| 15 | D | S | S | - | - | 45 | 38 | 83 | 844.44 | 10 (66.67) | 2 (13.33) |
| **Total-134** | | | | | | **339** | **271** | **610** | **799.41** | **83 (61.94)** | **12 (8.96)** |
| 5 | S | D | D | S | - | 17 | 15 | 32 | 882.35 | 3 (60) | 1 (20.00) |
| 4 | D | S | D | S | - | 14 | 12 | 26 | 857.14 | 3 (75) | 0 (0.00) |
| 7 | D | D | S | S | - | 23 | 21 | 44 | 913.04 | 5 (71.43) | 1 (14.29) |
| **Total-16** | | | | | | **54** | **48** | **102** | **888.88** | **11 (68.75)** | **2 (12.50)** |
| 5 | S | D | D | D | S | 20 | 21 | 41 | 1050 | 3 (60) | 1 (20.00) |
| 8 | D | S | D | D | S | 29 | 31 | 60 | 1068.97 | 6 (75) | 0 (0.00) |
| 4 | D | D | S | D | S | 17 | 18 | 35 | 1058.82 | 3 (75) | 0 (0.00) |
| 7 | D | D | D | S | S | 25 | 29 | 54 | 1160 | 5 (71.43) | 0 (0.00) |
| **Total-24** | | | | | | **91** | **99** | **190** | **1087.91** | **17 (70.83)** | **1 (4.17)** |

D = Daughter & S = Son.

**Table 6:** Child Preference of Spouses based on Educational Status

| Educational Status | No. of Father/ Mother | Total No. Children (Live + Death) | | | | Child Preference | | | |
|---|---|---|---|---|---|---|---|---|---|
| | | Boys | Girls | Total | Sex Ratio | Boys | Girls | No Matter | Up to God |
| Illiterate mother only | 46 | 95 | 78 | 173 | 821.05 | 38 (82.61) | 1 (2.17) | 1 (2.17) | 6 (13.04) |
| Illiterate father & mother both | 59 | 125 | 101 | 226 | 808 | 48 (81.36) | 1 (1.69) | 1 (1.69) | 9 (15.25) |
| Literate mother only | 4 | 7 | 6 | 13 | 857.14 | 2 (50) | 1 (25) | 1 (25) | 0 (0.00) |
| Literate father & mother both | 126 | 161 | 140 | 301 | 869.57 | 71 (56.35) | 22 (17.46) | 15 (11.9) | 18 (14.29) |
| Literate mother without standard | 27 | 46 | 39 | 85 | 847.83 | 19 (70.37) | 2 (7.41) | 1 (3.7) | 5 (18.52) |
| Literate mother (Class I-IV) | 65 | 73 | 61 | 134 | 835.62 | 38 (58.46) | 10 (15.38) | 8 (12.31) | 9 (13.85) |
| Literate mother (Class V-VIII) | 33 | 38 | 34 | 72 | 894.74 | 15 (45.45) | 9 (27.27) | 5 (15.15) | 4 (12.12) |
| Literate mother (Class IX-X) | 4 | 3 | 4 | 7 | 1333.33 | 1 (25) | 2 (50) | 1 (25) | 0 (0.00) |
| Literate mother (Class XI-XII) | 1 | 1 | 2 | 3 | 2000 | 0 (0.00) | 0 (0.00) | 1 (100) | 0 (0.00) |
| Literate mother (Graduate & above) | - | - | - | - | - | - | - | - | - |
| **Total Mother** | **235** | **388** | **325** | **713** | **837.63** | **159 (67.66)** | **29 (12.34)** | **18 (7.66)** | **23 (9.79)** |
| Illiterate father only | 4 | 7 | 6 | 13 | 857.14 | 2 (50) | 1 (25) | 1 (25) | 0 (0.00) |
| Illiterate father and mother | 59 | 125 | 101 | 226 | 808 | 48 (81.36) | 1 (1.69) | 1 (1.69) | 9 (15.25) |
| Literate father only | 39 | 83 | 64 | 147 | 771.08 | 27 (69.23) | 3 (7.69) | 5 (12.82) | 4 (10.26) |
| Literate father & mother both | 126 | 161 | 140 | 301 | 869.57 | 71 (56.35) | 22 (17.46) | 15 (11.9) | 18 (14.29) |
| Literate father without standard | 7 | 18 | 8 | 26 | 444.44 | 5 (71.43) | 0 (0.00) | 1 (14.29) | 1 (14.29) |
| Literate father (Class I-IV) | 61 | 104 | 86 | 190 | 826.92 | 42 (68.85) | 5 (8.2) | 5 (8.2) | 9 (14.75) |
| Literate father (Class V-VIII) | 71 | 91 | 79 | 170 | 868.13 | 38 (53.52) | 15 (21.13) | 12 (16.9) | 6 (8.45) |
| Literate father (Class IX-X) | 16 | 21 | 19 | 40 | 904.76 | 7 (43.75) | 3 (18.75) | 4 (25) | 2 (12.5) |
| Literate father (Class XI-XII) | 8 | 8 | 9 | 17 | 1125 | 2 (25) | 2 (25) | 3 (37.5) | 1 (12.5) |
| Literate father (Graduate & above) | 2 | 2 | 3 | 5 | 1500 | 1 (50) | 0 (0.00) | 1 (50) | 0 (0.00) |
| **Total Father** | **228** | **376** | **311** | **687** | **827.13** | **148 (64.91)** | **27 (11.84)** | **22 (9.65)** | **31 (13.6)** |

* Within the bracket the percentage are shown.

have a stronger correlation to proportion of more girl child than father (Table 6).

The sex ratio imbalance reflects an asymmetry of the survival. This asymmetry can be viewed as a case of violence against girl child. The case of violence indicates a clear cut low female-male ratio in the juvenile age groups primarily driven by excess female mortality in the age group 1-4 years and many cases during infancy. It is usually attributed to resource allocation inequality: the girl child given less food, breastfed for a smaller time span

**Table 7:** Sex-specific Child Mortality and Duration of Breastfeeding

| Duration of Breastfeeding (in Months) | Child Survival | | | | Child Mortality | | | |
|---|---|---|---|---|---|---|---|---|
| | Boys (%) | Girls (%) | Total (%) | Sex Ratio | Boys (%) | Girls (%) | Total (%) | Sex Ratio |
| 12 | 104 (29.46) | 118 (42.60) | 222 (35.24) | 1134.62 | 3 (12) | 26 (61.90) | 29 (43.28) | 8666.67 |
| 13-14 | 99 (28.05 ) | 77 (27.80 ) | 176 ( 27.94) | 777.78 | 10 (40 ) | 9 ( 21.43) | 19 ( 28.36) | 900 |
| 15-24 | 83 (23.51) | 54 (19.49) | 137 ( 21.75) | 650.60 | 7 (28) | 5 (11.90) | 12 ( 17.91) | 714.29 |
| 25+ | 67 ( 18.98) | 28 ( 10.11) | 95 (15.08 ) | 417.91 | 5 ( 20) | 2 ( 4.76) | 7 (10.45) | 400 |
| Total | 353 | 277 | 630 | 784.70 | 25 | 42 | 67 | 1680 |

and to make do with less and delayed health care. Table 7 indicates a less breastfeeding duration for girls than boys. As the duration of breastfeeding increases, the percentage of girls for each stage decreases more than boys.

A framework conceptualizing hypothetical mechanism by which the health and disease treatment process might produce the mortality differential among the people is related directly to the sex ratio. In the past near about all people took medicine from *ojha* (traditional medical practitioner). As a result both male and female suffer equally. However, after modern treatment, some of the people, especially males go to the modern health centers and majority of females have to go for *ojha,* local practitioner or home remedy (Table 8). As a result there is a large number of female death occurred in all age groups than the males. Table 8 also indicates the gender disparities for access over doctor/health centre for the population. The figure of females is always lower than males for each age group.

**Table 8:** Access over Doctor/Modern Medical Facilities

| Age Group | Doctor/Health Centre | | | |
|---|---|---|---|---|
| | Male | | Female | |
| | No. | % | No. | % |
| 0-4 | 46 | 82.14 | 29 | 59.18 |
| 5-9 | 46 | 80.70 | 26 | 52.00 |
| 10-14 | 57 | 82.61 | 22 | 47.83 |
| 15-19 | 42 | 76.36 | 20 | 40.82 |
| 20-24 | 35 | 81.40 | 10 | 16.67 |
| 25-29 | 40 | 71.43 | 14 | 31.11 |
| 30-34 | 22 | 57.89 | 12 | 26.09 |
| 35-39 | 25 | 78.13 | 10 | 25.64 |
| 40-44 | 23 | 67.65 | 4 | 33.33 |
| 45-49 | 20 | 64.52 | 6 | 23.08 |
| 50-54 | 12 | 48.00 | 1 | 05.56 |
| 55-59 | 4 | 33.33 | 0 | 0.00 |
| 60-64 | 2 | 25.00 | 0 | 0.00 |
| 65+ | 1 | 11.11 | 0 | 0.00 |
| Total | 375 | 71.43 | 154 | 34.15 |

Not only in disease treatment practices but also in maternal health care/treatment suggests dependency on treatment other than modern medical facilities during or after pregnancy Table 9. Table 9 also suggests a prevalence of maternal mortality

**Table 9:** 'Treatment of Mothers after Delivery' and Maternal Mortality

| Access over modern medical facilities | No. of Pregnancy | No. of children | | | | | | Maternal mortality |
|---|---|---|---|---|---|---|---|---|
| | | Live | | | Death | | | |
| | | Boys | Girls | Sex Ratio | Boys | Girls | Sex Ratio | |
| Yes | 639 | 284 | 169 | 595.1 | 21 | 10 | 476.2 | 2 |
| No | 218 | 69 | 108 | 1565.2 | 4 | 32 | 8000 | 11 |
| Total | 755 | 353 | 277 | 784.7 | 25 | 42 | 1680 | 13 |

to the female groups those not taken modern medical facilities during pregnancy.

The mortality represents a step forward in the analysis of sex ratio imbalances. The higher female mortality in both child and reproductive aged people are mainly responsible for the lower sex ratio. The excess female mortality would affect directly to

**Table 10:** Age Specific Male-Female Mortality Rate of the Population (Last 30 Years)

| Age Group | Male | Female | Total | Sex Ratio |
|---|---|---|---|---|
| 0-4 | 14 | 22 | 36 | 1571.43 |
| 5-9 | 7 | 12 | 19 | 1714.29 |
| 10-14 | 4 | 8 | 12 | 2000 |
| 15-19 | 2 | 3 | 5 | 1500 |
| 20-24 | 3 | 2 | 5 | 666.67 |
| 25-29 | 3 | 5 | 8 | 1666.67 |
| 30-34 | 5 | 8 | 13 | 1600 |
| 35-39 | 4 | 12 | 16 | 3000 |
| 40-44 | 3 | 7 | 10 | 2333.33 |
| 45-49 | 4 | 7 | 11 | 1750 |
| 50-54 | 4 | 10 | 14 | 2500 |
| 55-59 | 6 | 9 | 15 | 1500 |
| 60-64 | 4 | 7 | 11 | 1750 |
| 65-69 | 3 | 8 | 11 | 2666.67 |
| 70+ | 4 | 3 | 7 | 750 |
| **Total** | 70 | 123 | 193 | 1757.14 |

sex ratio of the population. Table 10 indicates an imbalance between mortality of two sexes. The higher death rate of females in respect of males of all age groups except two (Table 10) is due to disparity between them in the form of negligence to health care and improper nutrition, which affects female folk more brutally than their male counterparts.

## Observation

Men are the decision-makers for all aspects of women's lives. They want to be access better services within families as per availability, and it reflects on the sex-ratio pattern of the population. All together the sex-ratio of the reference population been relatively lower than natural and the lower status of women in the society is one of the major reasons of this deficit. The differential treatment methods for girl child might be due to their understanding and preferences of the differential survival capabilities of the two sexes. Restrictions on women's lives such as mobility and education have lead to barrier in visiting healthcare centers. Some scholars believed that to have a balanced sex ratio in the population, similar over-protective mechanisms seem to have operated at the social level with regard to male children. Nevertheless, over the centuries the additional care required for the male child becomes institutionalized as this having intrinsic social and religious value not possessed by the female child and preferential cultural practices. As well as the concept of the said society is like that, because of heavy hard working, males may have greater nutrition and health care facilities as females. For occupational structure, several occupational groups prefer more sons that reflect on expectancy of male child and results on negligence of female child as well as total female population. As a result excess female and child mortality would occur and which reflects on low sex ratio of the population. Beside these, very low sex ratio at birth also influences the overall sex ratio of the population. The cultural practices like son preference and health care practices including disease treatment pattern influence sex ratio of the population. A more demand of son influences sex ratio by declining the same.

However, the present situation of reference population is against the 'right to born' to female children, and their rights are violating in every step of life. To protect the rights of women through formulating governmental policy or government sponsored programmes is the best way to improve the overall condition of women. There is a need for alternative method for religious leaders and their communities to discuss 'equality of male-female' issues. Discussion between parents and adolescents during puberty must also be improved to provide them information before changes occur with their minds. Media messages and programs are alternative methods of reaching young women who are bound to their household or lack of attendance in school. Education increases the likelihood that woman will seek healthcare information and indistinguishableness between male-female. The location and maintenance of clinics in their areas must be addressed to ensure that there is an option for those that want it. Altogether, to follow-up these procedures may reduce the maltreatment to women in this population and facilitate them to gaining their real rights in near future.

## REFERENCES

Agnihotri, S.B. 1995. Missing Females: A Disaggregated Analysis. *Economic and Political Weekly*, 30(19): 2070-84.

Agnihotri, S.B. 2000. *Sex Ratio Pattern in Indian Population: A Fresh Exploration*. Sage Publication India Private Ltd., New Delhi.

Anuradha, K. and V. Uma 2002. Violence Against Woman. *Woman's Link*, 8(1): 2-4.

Basudev, S. 2003. Missing Girl Child. *India Today*, November 10: 14-20.

Bhat, P.N.M. 2002. On the Trial of Missing Indian Females. *Economic and Political Weekly*, 37(2): 5105-5118.

Census of India 2001. *Provisional Population Totals*. Govt. of India, New Delhi.

Chen, L.C. 1982. Where Have the Woman Gone? Insight from Bangladesh on Low Sex Ratio of Indian Population. *Economic and Political Weekly*, 17(10): 364-72.

Clark, A.W. 1987. Social Demography of Excess Female Mortality in India: New Direction. *Economic and Political Weekly*, 22(17): WS 12-21.

Clark, S. 2000. Son Preference and Sex Composition of Children: Evidence from India. *Demography*, 37: 95-107.

Dasgupta, M. 1998. *Women's Health in India: Risk and Vulnerability*. Oxford University Press, New Delhi.

Dyson, T. 1984. Excess Female Mortality in India, *Economic and Political Weekly*, 27(26): 422-26.

International Institute for Population Science 1995. National Family Health Survey: India. 1992-93. *International Institute for Population Science*, Bombay.

International Institute for Population Science 2001. National Family Health Survey: India. 1998-99. *International Institute for Population Science*, Bombay.

International Institute for Population Science 2001. National Family Health Survey: West Bengal, 1998-99. *International Institute for Population Science*, Bombay.

Jain, A.K. and Visaria, P. (ed.) 1988. *Infant Mortality in India: Differentials and Determinants*. Sage Publications Pvt. Ltd., New Delhi.

Karkal, M. 1987. Differentials in Mortality by Sex. *Economic and Political Weekly*, 12(32): 1343-47.

Krishnaji, N. 1987. Poverty and Sex Ratio: Some Data and Speculation. *Economic and Political Weekly*, 12(23): 892-97.

Millar, B.D. 1989. Changing Pattern of Juvenile Sex Ratios in Rural India, 1961-71. *Economic and Political Weekly*, 24(22): 1229-36.

Oldenberg, P. 1992. Sex Ratio, Son Preference and Violence in India: A Research Note. *Economic and Political Weekly*, 27(49-50): 2657-61.

Pal, M. Bharati, et al. 2002. Maternal Mortality in Rural West Bengal: Estimation of Its Rate and Identification of Underlying Causes. *Demography in India,* 34(2): 253-58.

Registrar General of India 1992. *1991 Census of India, Paper II of 1992, Table 2*. Registrar General of India, New Delhi.

Registrar General of India 1999. *Sample Registration System, 1998*. Registrar General of India, New Delhi.

Srinivasan, K. 1994. Sex Ratios: What They Hide and What They Reveal. *Economic and Political Weekly*, 19(51-52): 3233-34.

Srinivasan, K. 1998. *Basic Demographic Techniques and Applications*. Sage Publication, New Delhi.

Sundri, D. and Thombre, M. 1994. Declining Sex Ratio: An alternative analysis with special reference to Tamil Nadu State. *The Indian Economic Journal*, 43(4): 30-47.

Visaria, P. and Visaria, L. 1981. Indian Population Science after 1981 Census. *Economic and Political Weekly*, (Special Issue): 727-30.

# Protection of Child Rights: Concern, Issues and Reality

13

*Arpita Ghosh* and *Ahana Datta Mukherjee*

## Introduction

Children are the most weakest and vulnerable section of human population in any country since they are unable to raise their voice against those who injure them. The victimization of children in its different expressions is a constant feature of practically all societies. It is a common belief that childhood as currently understood is a relatively recent creation. In the old Roman days, the life of the young subjects was strictly monitored. Roman citizens were under the authority of a tutor up to puberty, which was deemed to occur at 14 for males and 12 for females.

Every nation developed or developing links its future with the status of the child. Childhood holds the potential and also sets the limit to the future development of the society. Children are the greatest gift to humanity. They provide eternal optimism and potential for human development. If the children are deprived of their childhood—economically, socially, physically and mentally—the nation gets deprived of the potential human resources for social progress, economic empowerment, peace and order, social stability and good citizenship.

## Protection of Child Rights under International Law

The advent of the Industrial Revolution brought about the enactment of child labour laws some of them dating back to the first half of the 19th century. It was then that the first conventions indirectly protecting children began in the international arena. Geneva Convention IV and the additional protocols incorporate and expand many of the principles contained in the Hague

Conventions and specifically provided for the protection of children. Articles 14 and 24 of the Geneva Convention IV and 76, 77, 78 of the Protocol, Article 50 of the Geneva Convention IV afford general protection of children as well as protects children in occupied territories. The Forced Labour Conventions of 1930 and the Abolition of Forced Labour Convention of 1957, require state parties to suppress and abolish forced child labour imposed by either the state or by the private individual and organizations.

The United Nations, its specialized agencies, non-governmental organizations and various other organizations of the UN have done pioneering work in protecting the rights of the child. The United Nations has adopted the Convention on the Rights of the Child in 1989. It can be mentioned here that any Convention on the Rights of the Child must be read within the framework of the International Bill of Rights, composed of the Universal Declaration of Human Rights, 1948, International Covenant on Civil and Political Rights (ICCPR), 1966 with its optional protocol and the International Covenant on Economic, Social, and Cultural Rights (ICESCR), 1966.

Article 25(2) of the Universal Declaration of Human Rights (UDHR) provides that childhood is entitled to special care and assistance. The International Covenant on Civil and Political Rights states that "every child shall have...the right to such measures of protection as are required by his status as a minor, on the part of his family, society and state". The General Assembly of the United Nations adopted a Declaration on the Rights of the Child in 1959 in which it declared that "the child by reason of his physical and mental immaturity, needs special safeguards and care including appropriate legal protection, before as well as after birth". Taking into account the various efforts made in this direction, the General Assembly adopted the Convention on the Rights of the Child on 20 November 1989 which entered into force on 2 September 1990 after requisite ratifications made under Article 49. India is a party to this convention which was ratified by it on 11 December 1992. As on June 2005, the Convention had 192 state parties. The Convention has 54 articles and is divided into three parts.

A number of rights have been stipulated in the Convention which includes the following:

- Right to life (Article 6, Para 1).
- Right to acquire nationality (Article 7).
- Right to freedom of expression (Article 13, Para 1).
- Right to freedom of thought, conscience and religion (Article 14, Para 1).
- Right to freedom of association and to freedom of peaceful assembly (Article 15, Para 1).
- Right to education (Article 28, Para 1).
- Right to benefit from social security (Article 26, Para 1).
- Right to a standard of living adequate for the child's physical, mental, spiritual and social development (Article 27, Para 1).
- Right to enjoyment of the highest attainable standard of health and facilities for the treatment of illness and rehabilitation of health (Article 24, Para 1).
- Right to the protection of the law against arbitrary or unlawful interference with his or her privacy, family, home or correspondence.
- Pre-natal and post-natal care for mothers [Article 24(2)(d)].
- Protection of the child from narcotic drugs (Article 33), sexual exploitation and sexual abuse (Article 34) and trafficking in children (Article 35).
- No child will be subjected to cruel, inhuman or degrading treatment or punishment or life imprisonment (Article 37).
- A child below 15 years of age is not to take part in hostilities (Article 38).

## World Summit for Children, 1990

The World Summit for Children was held on September 29 and 30, 1990 in New York to bring attention and promote commitment at the highest political level, to goals and strategies for ensuring the survival, protection and development of children as key elements in the socio-economic development of all countries and human societies. The Summit adopted the World Declaration on the survival, protection and development of children and the Plan of Action for implementing the World Declaration.

While the Declaration is a moral and joint commitment, the plan of action is a practical guide for national governments, international and non-governmental organizations to ensure the implementation of the Declaration's specific principles. The Action Plan sets specific goals for children and development in the 1990-2000 decade. Some of the goals are as follows:

- Reduction of under-five child mortality rate by one-third or 70 per 1000 live births, whichever is less.
- Reduction of maternal mortality rate by half.
- Reduction of severe and moderate malnutrition among under-five children by half.
- Universal access to safe drinking water and to sanitary means of excreta disposal.
- Universal access to basic education and completion of primary education by at least 80% of primary school age children.
- Improved protection of children in especially difficult circumstances.

However, children continue to pose a threat to the principles laid down in World Summit. For instances,

- More than one crore children under the age of five still die each year mostly from readily preventable diseases.
- Armed conflict killed more than 20 lakh children in the last years and left many other millions psychologically traumatized, disabled and even mutilated.
- An estimated three crore children are victimized by traffickers who almost invariably go unpunished.
- An estimated 15 crore children are malnourished.
- An estimated one child in three fail to complete five years of basic schooling.

- Over 10 crore are still out of school, 60% of them girls.
- Over 6 crore children work in the worst forms of child labour.

## Protection of Child Rights under Indian Law

India has a fairly developing model of legal order based on the democratic process with good popular response. The provision of Municipal Laws in India various safeguards and protections have been provided for the protection of children both by constitutional provision as well as other legislations, especially Indian Penal Code.

## Provision under Indian Penal Code

As per provision of Section 366A of the Indian Penal Code, whoever by any means whatsoever, induces any minor girl under the age of 18 years to go from any place or to do any act with intent that such girl may be or knowingly that it is likely that she will be forced or seduced to illicit intercourse with another person, shall be punishable with imprisonment which may extend to ten years and shall also be liable to fine.

As per provision of Section 373 of the Indian Penal Code, whoever buys, hires or otherwise obtains possession of any person under the age of 18 years with intention that such person at any age be employed or used for prostitution or illicit intercourse with any person or for any unlawful and immoral purpose, shall be punishable with imprisonment which may extend to ten years and shall also be liable to fine.

In addition to these, Section 376 of the Indian Penal Code can be invoked in providing punishment against child rape with imprisonment up to ten years and fine. Section 377 of the Indian Penal Code provides certain punishment against forceful intercourse amounting to ten years imprisonment and fine.

## Provisions under the Indian Constitution

Several provisions of the Constitution impose on the state a primary responsibility of ensuring that all the needs of the children are met and that their basic needs are fully protected.

Article 15 prohibits discrimination of citizens on the grounds of religion, race, caste, sex, place of birth or any of them. Clause 3 of the Article adds "Nothing in the article shall prevent the state from making any provision for women and children."

Article 23 prohibits traffic in human beings, forced work or extracting work without giving the minimum prescribed wages and declares them to be offences punishable in accordance with law.

Article 24 includes that no child below the age of fourteen years shall be employed to work in any factory or mine or engaged in any other hazardous employment.

The Directive Principles of State Policy in the Constitution also provides for several other provisions relating to the rights of children.

Article 39(a) imposes responsibility on the state that the health and strength of workers, men and women and the tender age of children are not abused and that citizens are not forced by economic necessity to enter associations unsuited to their age or strength.

Article 39(f) provides that children should be given opportunities and facilities to develop in a healthy manner and in conditions of freedom and dignity and youth should be protected against exploitation.

Article 45 provides that states shall endeavour for free and compulsory education for all children until they complete the age of fourteen years.

### Rights of Children Recognized under Various Legislations in India

There are more than 250 central and state legislations referring to children in India. Some of them have been adopted following the constitutional principles.

The Factory Act, 1948 prohibits employment of a child below 14 years in any factory. Restrictions have been imposed to safeguard the health of adolescent child workers between 14 to 18 years. Physical fitness certificate as well as periodical medical examinations (every 12 months) are required for those employed in factories. Child workers shall not be employed for more than four and a half hours a day and shall not be made to work in night shift.

The Mines Act, prohibits employment of children below 16 years of age in any part of the mining activities. A 'child' is defined as one below the age of 15 years. Those between 16 and 18 years can work in a mine if they are certified medically fit. Medical examination should be conducted every 12 months.

The Employment of Children Act, 1938 is meant to prevent employment of children in hazardous work. While children below 15 years are totally barred from the listed jobs, those between 15 and 17 may be employed subject to certain conditions.

The Motor Transport Workers Act, 1951 bans employment of children below 15 years. Adolescent between 15 and 18 years may be employed with medical certificate.

The Plantation Labour Act, 1951 prohibits employment of children below 12 years. Those who are between 12 and 18 years require medical certificate. Children below 14 years should not be asked to do night shifts.

The Apprentice Act, 1961 regulated the training of apprentices in industry. Children below 14 years cannot be given training. These are some legislation having prohibitionary approaches in child protection.

Recent trend of legislative protection of child has been drastically changed. To give protection to the Convention on the Rights of the Child, 1989 and to provide for the care, protection, treatment, development and rehabilitation of neglected and delinquent juveniles and for the adjudication of certain matters relating to the disposition of delinquent juveniles, the Juvenile Justice (Care and Protection of Children) Act, 2000 was enacted.

### Present Scenario of Child Abuse in India

In spite of various legislative sanctions especially under the Indian Penal Code and constitutional provisions as mentioned above in India incidents of child exploitation and abuse especially sexual abuse are not common and occurs in alarming way.

We here cite some recent case studies that struck our conscience from newspaper reports—

> Among the recent cases of child abuse, one of the most shocking incidents is that a female mathematics teacher allegedly shot video clips of her student after drugging and stripping them. The case revealed on 20th August, 2007. According to police, Uma Khurana used to call students for tuitions and used to offer lassi laced with drugs that would make them unconscious. Then two aides would help her to strip the girls and take pictures. The girls were threatened with severe consequences if they spoke out. Two girls told that Khurana even urged them to join prostitution.
>
> Female infanticide is another form of child abuse. One dreadful incident of child abuse took place in Chennai on 23rd March, 2007 where a girl child was being murdered by her mother Lakshmi. Lakshmi already had a daughter. So when she gave birth to a second girl child, she killed her. She admits that she refused to nurse her, to silence the infant's famished cries. The impoverished village woman squeezed the milky sap from an oleander shrub, mixed with Castor oil and forced the poisonous mixture down the newborn's throat. The baby bled from the nose and died soon afterwards.
>
> The Nithari serial killing in December 2006 is another form of child abuse. It left a bad taste for many families in Nithari village near Noida. Noida was for long haunted by incidents of kidnapping. On 29th December, 2006, when the police were investigating the kidnap of a teenaged girl, electronic surveillance brought them to an unoccupied house owned by Mohinder Singh. The electronic surveillance traced the cell phone of the kidnapped girl who was sexually assaulted and killed. But when the police investigation progressed, skeleton remains of many more children were found in sacks in the drain that was situated behind the house. This is when the case came to light. When the skeleton remains and objects found in the sacks were tested, it was found that they belonged to the

missing children. It was found that both Mohinder Singh and his servent Surinder Kohli were involved in kidnapping, sexually assaulting and killing of the missing children. Surinder acknowledged that he ate flesh of his victims. Organ trade was also suspected.

A 56-year old man raped his 8-year old niece in the absence of her parents. Ganesh Gorai, the accused and guilty crept into the girl's residence, lured her with chocolate after which he raped her and fled. The girl is in a serious condition.

On 29th May, 2007, healthy girl from a HIV affected family in Ammadi got admission into a higher primary school. This led to the parents of other students to transfer their children to other school.

Yesu Babu, aged 12 years of Vambay Colony in Vijaywada lost both his parents. His younger brother is HIV positive. Together they live with their grandmother in slum. Yesu is forced to work and is tortured at his workplace.

A 3-year old Sirisha who lost her parents due to HIV AIDS was sold to pimps and sexually assaulted. When the pimps found that her parents had AIDS, they left her and dumped her at a Hyderabad based NGO.

On August 14, 2007 at Chowgacha in Noida, a teacher of a school allegedly asked a class VII boy to pull down the pants of four of his classmates who had not done their homework.

A teenaged girl was sacrificed by her parents for a son. Raibhan Tembhurine, a school teacher and his wife Sarada killed their daughter Rachua.

A class IX student was beaten fifty-six times with a wooden ruler by his teacher because he sneezed in class. The boy Rajakumar Pasawan, was suffering from bruises and severe pain on his spinal chord due to the assault and had to be hospitalized. The teacher beat him, claiming that his sneezing was disturbing the class.

Buddhia Singh's coach and guardian Biranchi Das was arrested on August 13, 2007. Buddhia lodged a complaint against him stating that he slapped, hung him upside down from a ceiling fan and rubbed chilli powder in his eyes. Das also branded Buddhia with hot metal rod on his back and thigh.

## Conclusion

From the above discussion, it is clear that in India there is no dearth of legislation. In spite of these, both legislative and constitutional provisions, the need for judicial intervention has been immensely felt and judiciary, especially Apex judiciary has reacted sharply.

But here it may be mentioned that such judicial intervention is not sufficient enough to meet the necessities of time to control the exploitation of children. It has also been observed from various judgments of decided cases that in many cases at the time of pronouncing punishment for committing offense against the children, mainly in case of sexual offense, judiciary often give the lesser punishment in comparison with the gravity of offenses committed by the offender. In many cases, being shackled by the four corners of statutory and procedural compulsion and also due to lacunae in prosecution offenders have been awarded lesser punishment by the judiciary which is not at all encouraging in this regard.

But along with this changing attitude and view of the judiciary, especially that of Apex Court, some social changes are also necessary for the prevention and protection of children from sexual abuse and harassment. One of such changes, which is required is the economic upliftment and educational development of the poor, downtrodden and children of both economically and socially backward classes. It is also required to change the social thinking of such people and to control the population explosion, especially in this section of the society. Educational institutions have also to perform their duties and social obligations in this regard to protect the children by imparting social awareness and proper education to the children so that they may protect themselves and fight against these kind of social evils.

# Right to Information: An Instrument for Effective Participatory Development of the Indian Economy

14

*Ankita Ghosh*

One of the primary objectives of majority of nations vests in achieving economic development. Raising of income, well-being and economic capabilities of people is the most crucial social task that most of the nations targeted for. The key to success is in augmenting the planning task and properly hatching the plans for the thrust areas. Amongst all India also got the rhythm and adopted planning as the lever of social and economic change. Although the foundation is made by a fully centralized democracy in India, the 73rd and 74th Amendments of the Constitution in 1992 made a significant transit from a powerful centralised democracy to a power sharing closer to people governance—a shift from Lok Sabha to gramsabha. The gramsabha is mandated to approve all plans and programmes for social and economic development, audit the panchayat accounts and to select beneficiaries for all types of programmes (Bardhan and Mookherjee, 2006). The amendments also recognised the backward sections of the society (SCs and STs) and women through the reservation of seats in panchayati raj institutions and municipalities.

But centralisation and decentralisation are not either/or condition and an appropriate balance between the two is the pre-requisite for effective and efficient governance. This is the reason when national governments go for decentralising responsibilities they need to retain important policies and supervisory roles with them. On the other hand, effective decentralization advocates the enabling conditions that central authorities must create or maintain to allow local units of administration to take on more responsibilities.

Democratic decentralisation entails a system of governance in which citizens possess the right to hold local public officials to account through the use of elections, grievance meeting and other democratic means (Blair, 2000). In this type of governance the decision-makers and policy planners remain under the effective control of people and make a relationship between public officials and citizens in which the latter possesses a means of challenging and counterbalancing the arbitrary use of power (Agarwal and Ribot, 1999). However, according to Johnson (2003) accountability in this respect needs (i) an active citizenry; (ii) fiscal and political support from higher level authorities; and (iii) the existence of competitive political parties.

To restrict the misuse of power and to bring transparency and accountability in the system the Right to Information (RTI) act as approved by Indian Parliament in 2005 can be a strong and powerful instrument. The RTI allows people to demand any information held under the control of public authorities. The act contains the widest possible reach covering both central and state governments, panchayati raj institutions, local bodies and recipients of government grants. The RTI may stand as a big opportunity for the poor and marginal to make local institutions more accountable and counter the arbitrary use of power (Johnson, 2003) what Amartya Sen finds to be a momentous engagement with possibilities of freedom.

For India one of the big challenges in successful implementation of decentralisation vested in loosing the grip of central authority's power and make it pass to localities. Mainly India followed administrative decentralisation that mostly covers political decentralisation. It allowed people merely to vote, to propagate and to criticise. But where the target is overall economic development how the social and economic participation can be bypassed? As Amartya Sen says local democracy and decentralisation is not synonymous. In particular, decentralisation is not necessarily conducive to local democracy. In fact, in situations of sharp inequalities, decentralisation sometimes heightens the concentration of power and discourages rather than fosters participation among the unprivileged (Dreze and Sen, 2002). For India in different states the local authorities are seen to severely lack the fiscal autonomy and in effect it caused overwhelming dependency on government funding. Moreover, the problem became intense due to the inadequate supply of finance to the localities. Along with this the performance of gram panchayats remained so weak in many states that built a very different view regarding the usefulness of panchayats within people. In Madhya Pradesh, the panchayat is looked upon as a provider of only employment by a large proportion of people. Whereas in Tamil Nadu and Kerala only 60% and 50% of the people perceive panchayat to be useful for the actual reason of expressing views and needs and for implementing them (Bardhan and Mookherjee, 2006).

True participatory democracy needs a greater voice in decision-making either directly or through legitimate intermediate institutions (Bardhan and Mookherjee, 2006). For this transparency needs to be built on free flow of information and enough information should be provided to judge and monitor the allocation of developmental resources. Although in India, after a long period a comprehensive RTI law is enacted, it seems to fulfil the needs for an effective participatory democracy. However, the Act contains certain provisions that need to be reviewed. Specially how a law which is passed by the central parliament would be successfully implemented by the state authorities remains an open question till now.

## REFERENCES

Bardhan, Pranab and Dilip Mookherjee. 2006. *Decentralization and Local Governance in Developing Countries: A Comparative Perspective*. Massachusetts: MIT Press.

Dreze, Jean and Amartya Sen. 2002. *India: Development & Participation*. Oxford: Oxford University Press.

http://www.ifpri.org Imphal Free Press; posted 2005-05-28.

# Rights and Privileges in India: An Overview

15

*Shyamal K. Nandy* and *Dipak K. Adak*

Man struggled for existence against nature and his fellow men since the very beginning of human history. This caused conflicts among themselves, which paved the way for framing the rules and regulations for the safeguard of the oppressed. Human right is the basic rights of human being such as expression of thoughts, expression of freedom, expression of liberty without any discrimination. The concept of human rights in ancient India was based on wars. The ancient writings contained rules of warfare that were laid down in the legal texts such as the code of Manu (200 BC to AD 100), the *Mahabharat* (1000 BC), Kautilya's *Arthasastra* (300 BC) and others (Nirmal, 2000). Humanitarian ideas in India became popular from the beginning of the nineteenth century. There are several areas where Indian Penal Code was enacted during this period. Important among them are—the abolition of *Sati* (1829), slavery (1811) and female infanticide (1830).

According to Sundara Raj (2000):

> Social and economic rights are an essential part of human rights. These include the right of work, the right to form free trade unions, the right to social security, the right to an adequate standard of living, including food, clothing and shelter, the right to health, and the right to education.

India's Constitution-makers were of the opinion that the people should have the right to live a life of basic human dignity. Article 21 of the Constitution states that "the right to life ensures minimum conditions of living with human dignity". Supreme Court's interpretation on this Article states that "the right to life includes the right to live with basic human dignity and all that goes along with it; namely the bare necessities of life such as adequate nutrition, clothing and shelter over the head and facilities for reading, writing and expressing oneself in diverse forms".

It goes without saying that violation of fundamental human rights is frequent in our country. According to the Universal Declaration of Human Rights, fundamental human rights are violated when, among other things:

(i) A certain race, creed or group is denied recognition as a "person". (Articles 2 and 6)

(ii) Men and women are not treated as equal. (Article 2)

(iii) Different racial or religious groups are not treated as equal. (Article 2)

(iv) Life, liberty or security of person is threatened. (Article 3)

(v) A person is sold as or used as slave. (Article 4)

(vi) Cruel, inhuman or degrading punishment is used on a person. (Article 5)

(vii) Victims of abuse are denied an effective judicial remedy. (Article 8)

(viii) Punishments are dealt arbitrarily or unilaterally, without a proper and fair trial. (Article 11)

(ix) Arbitrary interference into personal, or private lives by agents of the state. (Article 12)

(x) Citizens are forbidden to leave or return to their country. (Article 13)

(xi) Freedom of speech or religion is denied. (Articles 18 and 19)

(xii) The right to join a trade union is denied. (Article 23)

(xiii) Education is denied. (Article 26)

## The Rights of Child

Exploitation of the child was common in many developing countries. The Human Rights Committee of Law, Asia, in Kuala

Lumpur has stated that child exploitation in the South Asian and South East Asian region is alarming and that the exploited children are totally defenseless. Under these circumstances, regional and international organizations such as Law Asia and the International Commission of Jurists have played an effective role in pressurizing the governments of developing countries to ensure implementation of the human rights of children in their territories. In India, the government as well as private organizations have been making efforts to check child labour. However, the problem lingers and evades a permanent solution (Chandrasekharan, 2000).

According to UN Declaration of the rights of the child (1959):

(i) The child is entitled to receive education, which shall be free and compulsory, at least in the elementary stages.

(ii) The child shall have full opportunity for play and recreation, which should be directed, to the same purpose as education.

(iii) The child shall not be admitted to employment before an appropriate minimum age. He shall in no case be caused or permitted to engage in any occupation or employment, which would prejudice his health, or interface with his physical, mental or moral development.

## The Rights of Women

Sridharan (2000) is of the opinion that millions of women in our country live in conditions of abject deprivation of, and attacks against, their fundamental human rights for no other reason than that they are women. In an age of third world sensitivities and western political correctness, cultural defensiveness continues to undermine both social and economic development. Females almost universally are consigned to participation in the reproductive process and perhaps to being considered as rewards or prizes for successful males. Most men in most societies still argue that these ranks are biological and genetic.

There are several laws related to women's rights in our country. Some of them are as follows:

(i) The Dowry Prohibition Act, 1961.

(ii) The Indecent Representation of Women (Prohibition) Act, 1956.

(iii) The Hindu Marriage Act, 1955.

(iv) Eve Teasing.

(v) The Medical Termination of Pregnancy Test Act, 1971.

(vi) National Commission for Women Act, 1990.

(vii) The Equal Remuneration Act, 1976.

### The Rights of Aged Persons

Human rights are universal, and civil, political, economic, social and cultural rights belong to all human beings, including older people. The Human Rights of the Aged are explicitly set out in the universal declaration of Human Rights, the International Covenants, the Convention on the Elimination of All Forms of Discrimination against Women, and other widely adhered to International Human Rights Treaties and Declarations.

The Human Rights of the Aged include the following:

(i) The human right to an adequate standard of living, including adequate food, shelter and clothing.

(ii) The human right to adequate social security, assistance, and protection.

(iii) The human right to freedom from discrimination based on age or any other status, in all aspects of life including employment and access to housing, health care, and social services.

(iv) The human right to the highest possible standard of health.

(v) The human right to be treated with dignity.

(vi) The human right to protection from neglect and all types of physical and mental abuse.

(vii) The human right to full and active participation in all aspects of political, economic, social and cultural life of the society.

(viii) The human right to full and effective participation in decision-making concerning their well-being.

Amnesty International is concerned that perpetrators of past human rights violations continue to enjoy impunity in India.

**Recent Amnesty International Reports—India: Five Years**

It includes the following:

(i) The bitter and uphill struggle for justice in Gujarat (AI Index ASA 20/007/2007).

(ii) Amnesty International condemns multiple bomb attacks in Mumbai (AI Index: ASA 20/017/2006).

(iii) Continuing concern over the safety of civilians, including adivasis, caught in escalating conflict in Chhattisgarh (AI Index: ASA 20/018/2006).

(iv) Concerns with Protection of Human Rights Act (AI Index: ASA 20/019/2006).

(v) Amnesty International condemns multiple bomb attacks in Malegaon, Maharashtra (AI Index: ASA 20/025/2006).

(vi) Continued detention two years after the repeal of POTA (AI Index: ASA 20/026/2006).

(vii) The Armed Forces Special Powers Act (AFSPA) Review Committee takes one step forward and two backwards (AI Index: ASA 20/031/2006).

**Discussion**

Human rights are today's buzzwords. In any democratic nation the rights of the individual are respected. These are to be exercised and enjoyed by all people. Without them, people cannot fully develop as human beings. Exploitation of child is common in our country. Even to this day Indian children are being engaged in the match industry of Sivakasi in Tamil Nadu, carpet industry in Uttar Pradesh, and many other establishments. Owing to parental poverty, children below 14 years work in these industries for long hours in miserable conditions and in an unhealthy condition. There is no doubt that women in our society are undergoing changes in their aspirations, perceptions, expectations and values. Even though women's problems generally command a high priority in contemporary Indian society, rural women are still to liberate themselves from centuries of psychological, economic and social discrimination. It is a wrong notion that women have to fight men in order to obtain their rights. The issue should be presented as a joint struggle for change in society.

*Manushi*, a women's magazine, gives down-to-earth and graphic descriptions of the condition of women's life in India. Girls tortured for dowry or burnt alive only indicate the stray instances that come to the notice of the authorities. Paras Diwan and Peeyushi Diwan in their path-breaking book, *Law of Marriage and Divorce* (1997), stated that apart from matrimonial offences, some marriages break down, and divorce by mutual consent seems the only way out. Both within the home and outside, sexual assault has become so common that the Supreme Court in Delhi Domestic Working Women's Forum instructed the National Commission for Women to make quick responses to such emergencies. The fact that violence against women occurs primarily in private has also meant that it has remained hidden from public view, with the consequence that the global incidence of such abuses has been obscured. Women themselves are often reluctant to report violence against them because of shame and the socio-economic pressure to remain in relationships. Men control women by two means. One is by sheer physical strength. The other more subtle and thereby more insidious means is by defining culture. Human culture consists of behaviour patterns acquired by individuals as members of a social group. The anthropologists conceive culture, which is learned rather than genetically endowed behaviour. If so, much behaviour can be learned and certainly altered in the best possible way. If culture remains unchanged, not only will women's rights be denied, but also a vast and potent resource will go untapped.

There are many committed organizations and non-governmental organizations (NGOs) in India working for the advancement of human rights in addition to government appointed agencies. The role played by them is praiseworthy.

Indian society consists of numerous social, linguistic, religious and territorial groups. The bulk of the Indian population lives in villages. There exists diverse nature of practice of rules and regulations regarding human rights. In this regard we may get the micro level understanding of the nature of human rights prevailed in our village societies through anthropological approach. Wherein, we may look into the matter keeping in view the notion of human rights at the center connecting it with other components of the society in terms of political activities, religious activities, economic activities, educational activities and so on.

This type of micro level understanding throughout intensive investigation may be corroborated with the macro situation of the human society at large. Certain rights and privileges may be considered unique which are regulated by the norms of the society itself in rural society. But that kind of understanding may not be expected in the urban society especially in the metro cities. The structural pattern differs heavily between these two spheres of human society in our country. In this sphere the anthropologists may play a significant role to understand the real situation through micro level understanding within a holistic framework.

## REFERENCES

Chandrasekharan, A. 2000. "Human Rights Awareness in Education." In: *Human Rights in India: Historical, Social and Political Perspectives*. Ed.: C.J. Nirmal, Oxford University Press, New Delhi.

Nirmal, C.J. 2000. *Human Rights in India: Historical, Social and Political Perspectives*. Oxford University Press, New Delhi.

Sridharan, I. 2000. "Practising Human Rights: A Feminist Perspective." In: *Human Rights in India: Historical, Social and Political Perspectives*. Ed: C.J. Nirmal, Oxford University Press, New Delhi.

Sundara Raj, M. 2000. "Awakening of Human Rights." In: *Human Rights in India: Historical, Social and Political Perspectives*. Ed: C.J. Nirmal, Oxford University Press, New Delhi.

# Human Rights: The Indian Experience

16

*Prasenjit Sarkar*

All human beings are born with equal and inalienable rights and freedoms which are essential for the human entity. Since the inception of early civilization, people were aware of these rights, though not under the name of human rights. Human rights became the burning global issue since World War II. Nations observed social cannibalism and brutal abuse of rights of man from the war which enforced them to be united at one point of agreement under the United Nations Organisation. From the legal obligations, international covenants and treaties came into existence for effective enforcement and protection of human rights, but unfortunately the violation is going on till date in every corner of the civilized world. India is not beyond that array. From time immemorial, India experienced many socio-economic and politico-cultural upheavals, simultaneously with foreign invasion, inequality, religious conversion, armed conflict, riot, displacement and many other horrifying situations related to violation of natural and civil rights. Consequently, concept of rights with its connotations have also changed with the changing situations. In ancient India righteousness was treated as a human right on the basis of *Varnashrama Dharma* as enshrined in the ancient scripts. But medieval India faced autocracy as a result of which right was subverted due to the inherent crisis of an Islamic state in a non-Islamic society. British rulers imported post-enlightened values, but could not overcome colonial arrogance and feelings of racial superiority which created a subversion of human rights. These varied experiences enriched and matured India to get at the present 'Free' state, i.e. largest democracy in the world. The Constitution of India, laws and judiciary provided and ensured human rights to its citizens but practically there is a note of interrogation regarding its degree and implementation. In this paper efforts have been made to discuss the concept, development and constitutional status of human rights with special reference to law as the protective measure in the Indian context.

## Civil and Human Rights: Concept and Emergence

Since the prehistoric period, ancestors of modern men were totally dependent upon nature and its resources. In order to satisfy the basic needs, they had to exert power on nature and they began to live in small groups to facilitate their endeavour. While one group tried to exert more power to achieve better fulfilment of their needs, the others tried to obstruct them, resulting in inevitable conflict. In order to maintain equitable distribution of natural resources, some form of social control was necessary for early men. This instability of the pre-social days, forced them to form civil society by their point of agreement as proposed by "Social-contract" theory[1] makers. In the Neolithic period a large number of people began to live in villages and abandoned a nomadic existence. Domestication of plants and animals led them towards more stability and complex, socio-economic life. Larger conglomerations provided them with safety and security simultaneously with conflicts and clashes, and for resolution, centralized authority was also developed in order to control its individuals and to compel them to behave in conformity with norms of the society. Thus, larger conglomerations of early men formed civil society which helped them to rule themselves as well as to enjoy equal amenities/ rights, specially in exploiting natural resources. These are the civil rights of man. But the rights which are appertained to man include intellectual rights, rights of mind and rights of acting as an individual for his own comfort and happiness. These rights should not be obstructive to for the other to enjoy the same rights. Without these rights, dignity of human being is completely denied. On the other hand, human rights are those rights, by virtue of which, one can enjoy maximum natural rights against any public authority or state.

People formed the public authority for their own interest; but rights were first enjoyed by the public authority. Nigerian jurist, M.A. Ntumy, who opined that ideas of justice, equality and human rights etc. are meant to serve the capitalist system.[2] Justice, Krishna Iyer states, "after all, law has no value autonomy, economic power subconsciously controls law making, law courts and the professions of the bench and the bar...."[3] This is the root cause of oppression for the common people. That is why, people had to fight against tyranny of the ruling powers, for which laws were created to bind the rulers. Gradually, common principles of rights were initiated and successively established the concept of human rights through British *Magna Carta* of 1215, Petition of Rights of 1628, Habeas Corpus Act of 1641, Bill of Rights of 1689, American Bill of Rights of 1793, Declaration of the Rights of Man and of the Citizens in France of 1789. These declarations gave impetus to codify the most famous United Nation's Universal Declaration of Human Rights of 1948 after Second World War. But in India, the concept of human rights was developed from the ancient culture.

## Evolution of Human Rights

From the evolutionary perspective, human rights came into existence for the ancestors of man. The concept of human rights was introduced by Maurice Cranston, "human rights is the twentieth century name for what has been traditionally known as natural rights or in a more exhilarating phrase the rights of man." Concept of rights is being changed through generations with the changing situations/conditions. Thus, the concept was developed in the present form of human rights after subsequent metamorphoses.

In the Indian context, ancient literature, *veda* declares equality among human beings where no individual can claim to be superior to others and equal right over food, water and other natural resources. In the *Bhagavad Gita* righteousness has been described as the essence of *dharma*. In the vedic era king or monarch was not above law and on violation, he could be punished like any other person. *Vasudhaiva Kutumbakam*—the whole world as one family, equality of brotherhood and respect for human dignity are the ultimate aims of the *Vedas*. In the *Mahabharata*, a great emphasis was laid to *Rajadharma* where kings were to act according to law and ethics as dictated in order to escape from political disorder, social chaos and injustice. War was considered to be *Dharmayuddha* where enemies never killed the sick or the wounded out of humanity. After a long period in the post-vedic age Samrat Ashoka being influenced by the teaching of *Lord Buddha*, worked extensively for the protection of human rights and happiness of the common people. Torture and ill-treatment of prisoners were strictly prohibited under his administration. He successfully established the *Welfare State* where people enjoyed the basic freedom.[4] The *Ashtadhyayi* concept of *Buddhism* clearly embodies concept of non-violence not only to nature but also to fellow humans. The concepts of *Jainism* are more stringent in the ideas of non-violence and furtherance of human rights. Irrespective of caste, creed and religion, people of ancient India thus, enjoyed human freedom, liberty and equality by and large.

During the pre-Mughal period, the Hindus *faced* a series of socio-political upheavals. The Muslim rulers imposed *Jazia* on the non-believers of Islam, a major discrimination against the Hindus. The Muslim rulers were fundamentalist, autocratic, theocratic, irresponsible and devoid of ideas of rule of law, justice and morality, a counter-product of human rights. But in the Mughal period, Akbar the Great brought some basic changes like tolerance and non-discrimination towards the Hindus. During Aurangazeb, corruption in judiciary was treated as a crime. Delayed justice causing loss to a party could be compensated by the judge himself. Accused person enjoyed the right to release on bail and even may be declared acquitted in case of benefit of doubt. Aurangazeb made earnest effort to convert the Kashmiri pandits to Islam. To fight against injustice, oppression and conversion ninth Sikh Guru Teg Bahadur and four sons of the Guru Gobind Singh, tenth Guru had to sacrifice their lives.[5] After a long turmoil great saints like Shankaracharaya, Ramanuja, Madhava, Tulsidas, Kabir, Nanak, Sri Ramkrishna and others appeared and reinterpreted the *vedic* values with their ideals and philosophy (mutual understanding, tolerance, human equality, etc.) with a view to establishing natural law with a flavour of religion. *Sufism* spread the message of equality and secularism to bind pluralistic society.

During the years 1765-93, there was a clear transition from the Muslim to British sovereignty in India. In 1765, English *East India Company* received the Diwani of Bengal, Bihar, Orissa from the *Mughal* Emperor Shah Alam after the battle of Buxar. This was the first instance where the English received legal authority for administration over parts of India. In 1793, Lord Cornwallis instituted Permanent Settlement in Bihar, thus formally inaugurating British rule in India. Under the early East India Company rule in India the revenue was usually collected by means of inhuman torture. Indian people witnessed unjust treatment under colonial rule in India. Some humanitarian ideas were honoured by the British Government, in the form of abolition of slavery in 1811, abolition of sati in 1829, abolition of infanticide in 1830, establishment of torture commission in Madras Presidency in 1855. But they exploited both the Indian masses and India economically, politically, culturally and spiritually. Political and civil liberties and rights of the Indian people were totally jeopardised. This destruction led the people to demand fundamental freedoms, civil and political rights. After a long struggle the British Cabinet Mission in 1946 recognised the need for a written guarantee of fundamental rights in the Constitution of India and envisaged a Constituent Assembly for framing the Constitution of India. Thus, meaning of right has been changed through time. This prolonged experience helped to codify the rights elaborately in the Constitution of India.

## Constitution of India and International Covenants

The Preamble to the Constitution of India refers to the promise of:

**Justice**—social, economic and political;

**Liberty** of thought, expression, belief, faith and worship;

**Equality** of status and opportunity; and to promote among them all;

**Fraternity** assuring the dignity of the individual and the unity and integrity of the nation.[6]

IN OUR CONSTITUENT ASSEMBLY 26th day of November, 1949, do HEREBY ADOPT, ENACT AND GIVE TO OURSELVES THIS CONSTITUTION.

Part III of the Constitution dealing with fundamental rights contains powerful provisions to combat all forms of discrimination, based on gender, race, caste or descent. Article 14 guarantees equality to all in a general way and grants equality before the law and equal protection of laws within the territory of India. Article 15 declares that the state shall not discriminate against any citizen on grounds only of religion, race, caste, sex or place of birth. Article 15(4) permits state to make special provision for upliftment of the citizens from the backward classes as well as scheduled castes and scheduled tribes. Article 16 provides equality of opportunity in the matters of public appointment with provisions for reservation in appointment and promotion in favour of any backward classes of citizens. Article 17 of the Constitution states to abolish untouchability.[7] In addition to the above, Constitution of India seeks to assure the constitutional ideals of equality and fraternity in particular, Articles 21, 23, 29(2), 38(2), 46, 325, 330, 333 and 335 under Indian Constitution to make the life of disadvantaged and marginalized citizens of society meaningful.[8]

Articles 36 to 51 laid under Part IV of the Constitution under the Directive Principles of State Policy cover a wide area of socio-economic and cultural justice. In democracy, the existence of fundamental rights depends upon socio-economic condition of people. This justice is the basis of establishing a *Rama Rajya* in India as dreamt by Mahatma Gandhi. Thus, different rights are provided and protected by the Constitution of India. But a stigma prevails over this fact which is that these rights are violated.

During World War II, nations around the world, witnessed the holocaust, Nazism, Fascism and other brutal abuse of human rights. Then nations decided to promote and protect human rights and freedom, and formed United Nations Organisation.

United Nations Charter (1945). Articles 55 and 56 cast a legal obligation to promote respect for the observance of human rights. Several charters and treaties came into existence for the effective enforcement of human rights.

Universal Declaration on Human Rights, 1948[9] declares, all human beings are born free and equal in dignity and rights....[10] Every one has the right to life,[11] right to property,[12] equal access to public services,[13] economic, social and cultural rights,[14] right to work, free choice of employment, just and favourable remuneration, to form and join trade unions, right to standard of life adequate for health and well-being of himself and his family and medical care in the event of unemployment, sickness, disability, etc.[15] and right to education.[16]

International Covenant on Civil and Political Rights, 1966[17] and its two optional protocols states, all the people have the right of self-determination,[18] equal right of men and women to enjoy all civil and political rights,[19] right to life which shall be protected by law,[20] right to liberty and security of person,[21] right to enter his own country[22] and recognition everywhere as a person before the law.[23]

International Covenant on Economic, Social and Cultural Rights, 1966[24] again declares the right of self-determination,[25] equal right, to men and women to enjoy socio-economic and cultural rights,[26] right to work,[27] social security[28] and education for every one.[29]

Constitution of India and international laws emphatically declares the right to life, equality from all the important dimensions of life and freedom, which are more or less common. In addition to the above other international and regional conventions like: European Convention on Human rights, 1950, European Social Charter, 1961; Helsinki Declaration, 1975; Geneva "Red Cross" Convention, 1949; Inter American Commission on Human Rights, 1960; American Convention on Human Rights, 1969; African Charter of Human Rights, 1981; and so many came into existence for the effective enforcement of human rights. In spite of having a lot of protective instruments, nobody is bound by International Human Rights Law.

## Law, Judiciary and Human Rights

India, like many other nations, is not interested to adopt the International Bill of Rights. Actually there is no such international code to bind or enforce a nation to protect human rights. India is a party to the International Covenant on Economic, Social and Cultural Rights and International Covenant on Civil and Political Rights, adopted by the General Assembly of the United Nations on the 16 December 1966. As a signatory the Government of India enacted The Protection of Human Rights Act, 1993[30] for the constitution of National Human Rights Commission, State Human Rights Commission[31] in the state and Human Rights Courts for the better protection of human rights and for the matters connected herewith or incidental thereto. Some other important legislations also enacted by the Union Government are, National Commission for Minorities Act, 1992; National Commission for Women Act, 1990; Protection of Civil Rights Act, 1955; Scheduled Castes and Scheduled Tribes (Prevention and Atrocities) Act, 1989; Immoral Traffic (Prevention) Act, 1987; Bonded Labour System (Abolition) Act, 1976; Juvenile Justice (Prohibition and Regulation) Act, 1986, etc. with a view to protect human rights in wider perspective.[32] Article 32 and 226 are the novel provisions in the Constitution of India[33] for the enforcement of fundamental as well as other legal rights of the individuals through judicial means.

Code of Criminal Procedure (hereafter Cr. P.C., 1973)[34] provides several human rights to the arrested person, the person arrested shall not be subjected to be more restraint than is necessary to prevent his escape,[35] to be examined by a registered medical practitioner,[35A] to be informed of grounds of arrest and of right to bail,[36] in case of female search shall be made by another female, with strict regard to decency,[37] to be produced before the Magistrate of the concerned jurisdiction without unnecessary delay,[38] except Magistrate Order,[39] in case of a female, medical examination shall be made only by or under the supervision of a female registered practitioner.[40] Accused person has the right to obtain all documents relevent to the charges formed against him, free of cost.[41] He also has the right to defend himself by a pleader of his choice[42] and right to legal aid if he has not sufficient means to engage a pleader. Accused also gets an opportunity to make representation against the punishment, before it is imposed.[43] Service of summons in the name of a female, in case of her absence, may be served by leaving one of the duplicates for her with some adult member of her family residing with her.[44] In case of execution of search warrant in a closed place where the person in charge is a woman, the search shall be made, by another woman with strict regard to decency.[45] In course of investigation no woman shall be required by a police officer to attend at any place other than the place in which such woman resides.[46] As regard to granting bail in case of non-bailable offences special provision is shown towards woman, i.e. arrested person may be released on bail, but, (i) such person shall not be released if there appears reasonable grounds of believing that he has committed an offence punishable with death or imprisonment for life; (ii) such person shall not be so released if such offence is a cognizable offence and he had been previously convicted of an offence punishable with death, imprisonment for seven years or more or he had been previously convicted on two or more occasions of a non-bailable and cognizable offence. Provided that the court may direct that a person referred to in clause (i) or clause (ii) be released on bail if such person is under the age of sixteen years or a woman or is sick or infirm.[47]

In case of dowry death when (i) the case involves suicide by a woman within seven years of her marriage; or (ii) the case relates to the death of a woman within seven years of her marriage in any circumstances raising a reasonable suspicion that some other person committed an offence in relation to such woman; or (iii) the case relates to the death of a woman within seven years of her marriage and any relative of the woman has made a request in this behalf; or (iv) there is any doubt regarding the cause of death; or (v) the police officer for any other reason considers it expedient so to do, he shall forward the body to the nearest civil surgeon for medical examination.[48]

If a woman sentenced to death is found to be pregnant, the High Court shall order the execution of the sentence to be postponed and may, if it thinks fit, commute the sentence to imprisonment for life.[49] Right to life of a (living) fetus is really honoured.

Some important tools against torture and confession caused by inducement, threat or promise when irrelevant in criminal proceeding,[50] confession to police officer not to be proved,[51] confession by accused while in custody of police not to be proved against him and the person arrested not to be detained more than twenty-four hours[52] except[53] a special order from the Magistrate under Section 167 Cr. P.C. Except these, judiciary protects human rights through some legendary verdicts against custodial torture, solitary confinement, handcuffing, illegal arrest and detention, common police lock-up in case of female suspects and also in favour of free legal aid to disabled prisoner, speedy trial and to get compensation in the case of established violation of fundamental right to life.[54]

## Conclusion

Codified words regarding human rights in the form of acts or statutes are meaningless unless codes are implemented. The codes are implemented by the National Justice System in India. Justice Krishna Iyer said, "The access to Justice is a foremost human right." The Human Right Commission has no power to give an authoritative judgment in respect of offences arising out of violation of human rights. It is nothing but a recommending authority. Being influenced by different factors (e.g. sponsorship, fear of retribution, etc.) recommendation and its proper implementation is a crucial problem undoubtedly. Its main function is to promote awareness of human rights, research, review of law and violating factors related with human rights, and recommendation for remedial measures, spread of human right literacy, encourage the efforts of NGOs working in the field of human rights and such others as it may consider necessary for the promotion of human rights. Activities of the National and State Human Rights Commission have not always been up to the desired mark. Main constraints in this regard are lack of human rights education of the common people as well as of law enforcing agencies. For awareness as well as better protection it may be incorporated in the secondary level school syllabus.

*Panchayats* may also adopt awareness programmes for the common people in the rural areas. Amendments to the Constitution and existing law are required so that the commission can investigate the complaints while the state shall provide sufficient infrastructure needed in this regard.

## NOTES

1. H.N. Banerjee (1990). Introduction to Social Cultural Anthropology.
2. S. Guha (2003). Human and Civil Rights: Perspective and Practice with Special Reference to India.
3. Cranston, Maurice. (1962). What are Human Rights?
4. S. Deshta and L. Dadwal (2005). Genesis of Human Rights in India.
5. Sarkar, J.N. (1920), Mughal Administration.
6. S.S., Chakraborty and N. Pramanik (1983). Bharater Shasan Byabastha-O-Rajniti.
7. Justice A.S. Anand (2005). The Constitutional Model of Equality and Fraternity: The Indian Experience.
8. Articles 14, 15, 15(4), 16, 17, 21, 23, 29(2), 38(2), 46, 325, 330, 335 of the Constitution of India.
9. Universal Declaration of Human Rights, 1948.
10. Article 1 of Universal Declaration of Human Rights, 1948.
11. Article 3 of Universal Declaration of Human Rights, 1948.
12. Article 17 of Universal Declaration of Human Rights, 1948.
13. Article 21(2) of Universal Declaration of Human Rights, 1948.
14. Article 22 of Universal Declaration of Human Rights, 1948.
15. Article 23 of Universal Declaration of Human Rights, 1948.
16. Article 25 of Universal Declaration of Human Rights, 1948.
17. International Covenant on Civil and Political Rights, 1966.
18. Article 1 of International Covenant on Civil and Political Rights, 1966.
19. Article 3 of International Covenant on Civil and Political Rights, 1966.
20. Article 6(1) of International Covenant on Civil and Political Rights, 1966.
21. Article 9(1) of International Covenant on Civil and Political Rights, 1966.
22. Article 12(4) of International Covenant on Civil and Political Rights, 1966.
23. Article 16 of International Covenant on Civil and Political Rights, 1966.

24. International Covenant on Economic, Social and Cultural Rights, 1966.
25. Article 1 of International Covenant on Economic, Social and Cultural Rights, 1966.
26. Article 3 of International Covenant on Economic, Social and Cultural Rights, 1966.
27. Article 6 of International Covenant on Economic, Social and Cultural Rights, 1966.
28. Article 13 of International Covenant on Economic, Social and Cultural Rights, 1966.
29. Article 14 of International Covenant on Economic, Social and Cultural Rights, 1966.
30. The Protection of Human Rights Act, 1993.
31. The Protection of Human Rights (Amendment) Act, 2006.
32. A Panel of Legal Commentators (2006) Law relating to Human Rights.
33. Articles 32 and 226 of the Constitution of India.
34. Code of Criminal Procedure, 1973.
35. Section 49 of Cr. P.C.
35A. Section 54 of Cr. P.C.
36. Section 50 of Cr. P.C.
37. Section 51(2) of Cr. P.C.
38. Section 56 of Cr. P.C.
39. Section 167 of Cr. P.C.
40. Section 53(2) of Cr. P.C.
41. Sections 207 and 208 of Cr. P.C.
42. Section 303 of Cr. P.C.
43. Sections 235(2) and 248(2) of Cr. P.C.
44. Section 64 of Cr. P.C.
45. Section 100(3) of Cr. P.C.
46. Section 160 of Cr. P.C.
47. Section 437 of Cr. P.C.
48. Section 174(3) of Cr. P.C.
49. Section 416 of Cr. P.C.
50. Section 24 of Indian Evidence Act, 1872.
51. Section 25 of Indian Evidence Act, 1872.
52. Section 57 of Cr. P.C.
53. Reddy, Ramachandra K. (2005). Protection of Human Rights in the Administration of Criminal Justice.
54. Lahiri, S.K. (1995), *Police Handbook*, Vol. 1.

# International Human Rights Law

17

*T.R. Maruthi*

## Introduction

Traditionally individuals were under the exclusive jurisdiction of the State of which they were nationals and where they lived. No other State could interfere with the authority of that State, which in a way had a sort of right and death over those individuals. From one perspective, the modern development of international law has been a remarkable success. The general opinion is that violations of international human rights law are not due to the inadequacy of its rules. Rather, they stem from an unwillingness to respect the rules, from insufficient means to enforce them, from uncertainty as to their application in some circumstances and from a lack of awareness of them are the part of the general public. The international human rights law, like anybody of law, is not static, and it must always be interpreted and applied in such a way as to uphold its basic objectives and relevance. A human right, as a concept, is but one device of many for thinking about the real, but a vital device nonetheless.[1] Due to the weak record of ratification of key human rights treaties, many of the problems accord in the image of contemporary human rights law. Furthermore, lack of national implementation of legislation is one of the greatest setbacks in the history of human rights protection. Basically, the value of human rights is largely tested by their implementation.

The effective application of international human rights law requires planning and preventive actions. Moreover, lack of awareness/understanding by authorities and different legal system and constitutional arrangements in region common and civil, dualist and monist approaches that exact content and nature of this application of international human rights are not comfortable in the present scenario. Of course, the lack of commitment, political considerations, lack of international enforcement mechanisms, etc. are also to be considered as major impediments of these intrinsic, instrumental, natural and basic tights of human being. This article makes an attempt to give more information relating to human rights and its different facets with international humanitarian law, terrorism, regionalism, and postmodernism. Rights come into existence only if their subjects exist; and they will be effective if someone exist to respect them. This versatile concept reflects on the realities of societies that are either torn apart by gross human rights violations, or envisioned utopian societies that would 'really' be at peace with their cultural diversity. Although the existence of human rights could be attributed to their rigorous protection by international judicial agencies and advocates in the field, we can run the risk of overemphasizing human rights as law.

## International Humanitarian Law

International humanitarian law, also known as the law of war, the laws and customs of war or the law of armed conflict, is the legal corpus comprised of the Geneva Conventions and The Hague Conventions, as well as subsequent treaties, case law, and customary international law. Since the adoption of Geneva Convention of 1949 mankind has expressed number of armed conflicts affecting almost every continent. Humanitarian law places constraints on the waging war. Its impacts ultimately depend on whether its rules are actually applied in times of conflicts.[2] The measures must be taken for the implementation of international humanitarian law are complex and involve many sphere of government activity and sector of public life. The international humanitarian law has long history as compared to international human rights law. Basically, the humanitarian law is applicable during war period. Four Geneva Conventions and Additional Protocols of 1977[3] have provided legal protection. Even so, there have been numerous violations of these treaties, resulting in suffering and death which might have been avoided had international humanitarian law been better respected.

Prisoner of war must all times be humanly treated. Any unlawful act or omission by the detaining power causing death or seriously endangering the health of a prisoner of war in its custody is prohibited, and will be regarded as a serious breach of the Geneva Convention relating to the Prisoner of War of 1949. Article 17 states that no physical or mental torture, nor any other form of coercion may be inflicted on prisoners of war to secure from them information of any kind.

Article 27 provides that protected persons are entitled, in all circumstances, to respect for their persons, their honour and their family rights. And also they shall at all times be humanly treated and shall be protected especially against all acts of violence or threats thereof and against insults and public curiosity. Article 10 of the 1977 Additional Protocols to the Geneva Convention, 1949 states that all the wounded and sick and shipwrecked, to wherever party they belong, shall be respected and protected. Furthermore, in all circumstances they shall be treated humanly and shall receive, to the fullest extent practicable and with the least possible delay, the medical care and attention required by their condition. Article 75 of the above stated Protocol provides that the following acts are and shall remain prohibited at any time and in any pace whatsoever, whether committed by civilian or by military agents:

A violence to the life, health, or physical or mental well-being of persons, in particular—

1. murder;
2. torture of all kind, whether physical or mental;
3. corporal punishment; and mutilation.

The great majority of the provisions of the Geneva Conventions, including common Article 3 are considered to the part of customary international law. Furthermore, given that there are now 192 states to the Geneva Conventions,[4] they are binding on nearly all states as a matter of treaty law. The numerous treaty of humanitarian law express the continuing concern of the international community to maintain and preserve fundamental rules in the specific context of armed conflicts where the rule of law[5] is particularly threatened. Humanitarian law can therefore be regarded as a species of the broader genus of human rights law. This is not a destination in terms of their intrinsic nature, but a destination based on the context of application of rules designed to protect human beings in different circumstances.

### Terrorist Activities

A gunman assassinates an American NATO employee in Turkey. A car bomb explosion kills a high-level government official on a busy street in Sri Lanka. Government troops murder eleven civilians in a village in Uganda. A Palestinian man stabs four Israeli women to death in Jerusalem. A clash between police and African National Congress supporters results in twelve deaths, including that of a twelve-year-old boy and a nine-year-old girl. A United States Stealth aircraft releases a bomb that kills over four hundred Iraqi civilians in a Baghdad shelter. International terrorism is the closest thing to the military-related dimension of security. It is a menace to peace and security and it strikes in a stealthy and vicious manner.

These incidents, and numerous others that occur regularly, underscore the fact that politically related violence, ranging from spontaneous individual acts to organized warfare, is a pervasive feature of worldwide politics. Under the analytical framework presented, impermissible political violence consists of acts committed by government or private actors who violate fundamental human rights without justification or excuse. Human rights, humanitarian law, and international legal norms restricting the use of force as a means of dispute resolution presently contain the means to construct an effective and morally compelling framework to define the contours of impermissible political violence.[6]

The Tokyo Convention, The Hague Convention, and the Montreal Convention—address violence directed against aircraft and air passengers. All three reflect a solid international consensus among states that hijackings, bombings, and other attacks on commercial aircraft pose a serious problem to international transportation.[7]

The rationale for creating an international criminal offense for hijacking rests on the ostensibly neutral goal of protecting international transport. Private actors, however, may perceive two reasons why this goal is not neutral. First, only states, or large corporate entities as agents of states, own and possess aircraft. To private actors who seek redress for their political grievances, they are tangible symbols of state power. Private actors who are unable to achieve humanitarian or human rights objectives through peaceful means may perceive no reason to subordinate their interests to states' interests in safe international travel.

The fact that terrorism exists indicates that many politically aggrieved groups feel that they are without a voice to air their grievances. Human rights are more of a reality in the papers of international human rights conventions than they are in the lives of millions of people. Despite the complex and varied reasons why state and private actors engage in violent acts, it is indisputable that injustice breeds violence. Where widespread and systemic injustices exist, actors may permissibly resort to violence. The international community needs to address the underlying causes of these injustices, and punish states as well as private actors for acts of *per se* impermissible violence.

Substantive criminal law and customary international law, evidenced by, among other things, the complex of international treaties on such conduct as hijacking, hostage taking, human rights, the laws of war in international and civil strife, and general principles that are derived from the domestic laws of virtually all nations, render certain conduct criminal. All states and organizations agree on the condemnation of the heinous and despicable phenomenon of terrorism. Even states that pay only lip service to this condemnation would never admit that they either support or condone terrorists. To what extent do international standards on human rights and humanitarian law make rebellion legitimate? Do these same standards allow rebels to resort to terrorist methods?

A review of international instruments on human rights and the whole body of international humanitarian law of armed conflict demonstrates how rebellion and terrorism are appraised. Specific treaties on terrorism, recently concluded under the auspices of some international organizations, are not included in this review because they have not yet attained universal application or because they deal only with a specific issue. Under consideration are universal norms and declarations.

Terrorism should not be used as a pretext for curtailing human rights. Restrictions on human rights for the purpose of a more efficient fight against terrorism are warranted only under strict conditions. At the same time, one of the fundamental purposes of the contemporary international human rights regime is to serve as a bulwark against excesses not just to protect the minority from the majority and the vulnerable from the powerful but to serve as powerful limitations on the power of government in times of stress and confrontation, when the risks of excess and over-reaction are sharpest.

The direct impact of terrorism is clearly illustrated by its immediate consequences. These consequences usually fall into three categories of violations: the right to life, liberty, and dignity of the individual. Terrorist acts include, but are not limited to, murder, kidnapping, and seriously injuring innocent parties, which all deny victims their human rights to life, liberty, and dignity. Additionally, a human rights approach is consistent with the emerging understanding that massive human rights abuses may justify piercing national boundaries. Increased globalization creates a greater ripple effect with respect to human rights violations. A multilateral response to terrorism utilizing a tripartite approach is pragmatic, morally desirable, and consistent with ongoing efforts of the United Nations and trends in international public law, international counter-terrorism, and international human rights law.

The issue of terrorism is not a new one on the human rights agenda. For many years, acts of terrorism in all forms have endangered and killed innocent people, jeopardized fundamental freedoms and seriously impaired the dignity of human beings. States have therefore long been under an obligation to take measures to protect the fundamental rights of everyone within their jurisdictions against terrorist acts.

Human rights, along with democracy and social justice, are seen as a means to prevent terrorism. Thus, on this view, the key to enhancing security is the pursuit by all governments of a comprehensive human rights programme. The article gives a brief, general outline of human rights violations as a major causal factor of terrorism, followed by an analysis of human rights violations by acts of terrorism. Finally, and most importantly, the article considers human rights violations by counter-measures in the aftermath of September 11, and highlights the requirement for a balance between human rights and security. Whether or not violations of human rights are recognized as a major causal factor of terrorism has a bearing on the strategy adopted for fighting terrorism. This became very clear in the light of September 11. Almost all the principal human rights instruments contain language creating positive obligations human rights abuses.

The UN Commission on Human Rights, for example, has already determined that rape by non-state actors constitutes a violation of the rights of women. The same body also reiterated that 'the individual has the responsibility to strive for the promotion and observance of human rights'. A similar line of reasoning is evident in the International Covenant on Civil and Political Rights. Respect for human rights and fundamental freedoms are the rule; derogations are an exception to the rule. Some rights, for example, the right to life, freedom of thought, conscience and religion, and freedom from torture or cruel, inhuman or degrading treatment, and the principles of the precision and non-retroactivity of criminal law, may not be derogated from at all. The response to terrorism ought to be based on a holistic and inter-related understanding of human security, human rights, and human development—and all within the human rights and the rule-of-law framework.

This is a significant challenge and herein lays the core of the problem. The contemporary nature of threats in the form of catastrophic terrorism caused by suicide bombers or others who are systematically engaged in committing similar acts are indeed acts of terrorism. Respect for international law, international human rights law and international humanitarian law should be emphasized so that multilateralism remains the approach to fight global terrorism. International institutions need to be empowered. The fight against terrorism should take place at different levels.

### Universalism

The UN soon realized the best way to make member states accountable to their citizens would be to draw up detailed treaties which place obligations on states to protect the human rights defined in the UDHR. In 1966, after years of painstaking negotiations, the UN adopted two covenants which elaborate in more detail the human rights set out in the UDHR: the International Covenant on Civil and Political Rights and the International Covenant on Economic, Social and Cultural Rights. Taken together with the UDHR, these documents are sometimes known as the International Bill of Rights.

### International Criminal Law

International criminal law is the law that governs international crimes. It may be said that this discipline of law is where the penal aspects of international law including that body of law protecting victims of armed conflict known as International Humanitarian Law and the International Aspects of National Criminal Law.[8] The International Criminal Court has jurisdiction over four categories of crimes: genocide, crimes of against humanity, war crimes and aggression in both the preamble to the statute and in Article 5, these are variously described as 'the most serious crimes of concern to the International Community as a whole.'[9] Elsewhere, the statute describes them as 'unimaginable atrocities that deploy shock the conscience of humanity, international crimes, and the most serious crimes of international concern.'

The UN and the international community should not be lulled into thinking that justice will come to Rwanda with an 'effective' International Criminal Tribunal for Rwanda (ICTR), which has succeeded in securing custody of 45 inductees out of the total number of 53. This organ of international law seeks to apply the principles of fairness, due process, and justice to acts committed in the course of war,[10] whether civil or international. But how effective is it and other similar bodies in delivering justice? Are they simply a means of "victors justice"? Are the accused treated fairly? These are all legitimate questions. While certainly these institutions are a substantial boost for human rights around the globe, there are still several problems with them. One of the greatest concerns deals with the applicable body of law. In the statutes of the ICTY and the ICTR, a considerable amount of attention is paid to the prosecution, the judges, and the registry, as well as the enumeration of the crimes within the courts' jurisdiction.

There can be no question that the inclusion of defenses in the sphere of international criminal law constitutes an important stage in the recognition of the principle of fairness in international litigation and therefore the application of human rights standards in international criminal proceedings. Essentially, since militaries are built on a hierarchical structure that is to be rigidly adhered to, lower-ranking members of the armed services do not have the necessary intent or motive required for most crimes. A very closely related concept, though not a defense, is the notion of command responsibility.[11]

Although the laws of war are frequently altered after major conflicts, the post-Cold War revision of these rules has not occurred as a result of treaty negotiations. It has, instead, resulted from the United Nations Security Council's decision to create two temporary, *ad hoc* tribunals and from these courts' ensuing judicial decisions. The tribunals' transformation of the laws of war provides an opportunity to assess one of the most striking phenomena of international politics in the past ten years. It argues that international judicial law-making is most appropriate when the relevant underlying treaties are old, where underlying conditions have changed, and where there is little prospect for the treaties' revision. The phrase "human rights" was rarely mentioned in the 1949 Diplomatic Conference. The post-World War II period, however, saw great development in the human rights movement and the drafting of many new treaties that address states' treatment of their citizens. In 1968, the International Conference on Human Rights at Tehran called for the revision of the Geneva and Hague Conventions "to assure the better protection of civilians, prisoners and combatants in all armed conflicts". The latter phrase was a clear reference to the failure of the existing treaties to address civil wars. In response, the International Committee for the Red Cross, in consultation with experts and government representatives, drafted two treaties for the purpose of enhancing the 1949 Geneva Conventions and extending some of their provisions to civil wars. These treaties were the subjects of a Diplomatic Conference convened by the Swiss Federal Council in February 1974. Although the 1949 Conventions were drafted in a single year, the 1974 conference included many more states and was far more divisive. It convened for three yearly sessions, concluding only in 1977.

The most recent transformation of the laws of war has proceeded in three distinct stages: (i) the Security Council's decision to establish the ICTY and ICTR,[12] (ii) the subsequent reorientation of the Geneva Conventions undertaken by the ICTY judiciary, and (iii) the codification of those developments by states in the negotiations of the ICC treaty. Viewing this process over time, the ICTY judiciary's law-making emerges as the key transitional stage. It brought the Geneva Conventions to life through the adjudication of actual cases, it changed the definition of armed conflict in a way that lowered the threshold for applying laws that govern international conflicts and enhanced the regime governing civil wars. By so doing, it paved the way for the codification of these solutions in the ICC. The ICC has become a central symbol of the trans-Atlantic battle between Europe and the United States.

The outcome of the conflict for international criminal law is far from assured. The United States is currently waging a strong rear-guard action against the ICC.[13] Individuals are the principal actors dealt with by the statute, and they tend to be cast in the role of perpetrator. Humanity is the largest group allowed for, and, in a very idealized sense, humanity can be both victim and judge. Groups smaller than 'humanity' have more complex roles. National, ethnical, racial or religious groups can be the specific victims of crimes, and are in fact required to be the victim for the successful prosecution of genocide and crimes against humanity. These groups are of course comprised of individuals, yet something aside from the sum total of people, something shared between the current members of the group and their historical forebears, is seen as relevant to their victim status. During the First World War there was significant demand in Britain for 'Germany' to be punished for making war (in breach of international treaties) as well as for individual Germans to be tried for war crimes.

The US was hostile to this idea, arguing that responsibility for breaches of treaties and crimes against the laws of humanity were an issue for morality and not law. This view of the limits of law is still popular with some in US politics, and with many in the field of International Relations, but has long since been superseded in the dominant international criminal law discourse by a view that law is a way to realize morality across borders. International criminal law on this view represents a universal declaration of right and wrong in the international moral sphere. The atrocities of the Second World War presented such a challenge to Western ideas of progress and civilisation that a response had to be found. Part of this response has been the elaborate construction of an individual international agent to hold responsible for international crimes. Necessary to support this construction is the fiction of a global moral community peopled by rational individuals who act freely according to a shared ethical code.

## Regional Efforts

Regionalism is as old as history. Moreover, what is special in present regional arrangement is that their significance in integration of states has become very high. The European human right system is an innovative arrangement having supra-national authority. The regional arrangements are also possible avenues for the enforcement of the norms of United Nations and UN-related treaties.[14]

In sum, development regionalism contains the traditional arguments for regional cooperation such as territorial size and economies of scale, but, more significantly, add some which are expressing new concerns and uncertainties in the current transformation of the world order and world economy. During the Cold War a common argument (the "common security" approach) against nuclear armament. International human rights protection is seen either as a universal issue or as a regional one. There is little middle ground. It is on this neglected middle ground that the greatest possibility of improving the international system for human rights protection exists. By utilizing the strengths of both universal and regional approaches, the possibility of creating a system of protection able to identify and respond to the crucial issues at hand appears much stronger.[15] At its creation, the UN was seen as a way to a worldwide solution for human rights protection. It was hoped that a universal body could promote peace and security throughout the world and protect the human rights of individuals through universally established standards and programmes.

The idea at the time was to have the UN as the leading universal body, and that any form of regionalism had to be subordinate to the UN system. In order to test the argument that there is a worldwide process of rationalizations taking the shape of a new regionalism, it might have been simpler to choose another example than Asia-Pacific. East Asian regionalism is often described as *de facto* regionalism, whereas regionalization is supposed to take place *de jure* in Europe and North America. This contrast may be due to differences in political culture, but an alternative explanation could lie in the fact that the inter-state relations in East Asia are rather tense and unsettled.

The UN Charter Chapter VIII makes provision for regional arrangements in relation to peace and security. But it is silent as to human rights co-operation at the regional level. Nevertheless, the council of Europe moved as early as 1950 to adopt the European Convention on Human Rights. In 1969, the Analogous American Convention was adopted. Then African Charter of Human Rights and People's Rights was adopted in 1981. The question of regionalism was important for the United Nations at the time of its drafting and continues today. At its creation, the UN was seen as a way to a worldwide solution for human rights protection. The idea at the time was to have the UN as the leading universal body, and that any form of regionalism had to be subordinate to the UN system. The UN is involved in a wide array of issues, of which human rights is only a small part. It would be unfair to blame the UN for not creating an effective system of international human rights protection. The task of doing so is much too great for any one organization to undertake alone. From the above pros and cons of regionalism, it is visible to see both the extreme sides. However, the regionalism arrangement should go hand in hand with global arrangement on the issue of human rights.

The regional arrangement will fill some of the lacunas of the universal mechanism in the promotion and protection of human rights. For instance, since there is socio-cultural tie between states of the same region, it is easier to formulate and implement human rights norms. On the other hand, the global mechanism will help in fixing minimum standards for all human beings. It has generated the more extensive jurisprudence than any other part of international system. The preservation of human rights has become a major function, embodied for example in the Council of Europe and the European Court of Justice, where states can be brought to the bar for human rights violations. The very purpose behind the establishment of Organization of African Unity (OAU) was to deal with problem of colonialism and its vestiges, with apartheid in South Africa, Namibia and Rhodesia (now Zimbabwe) and the economic development of post-colonial African states. In 1979, the OAU decided to draft an African Charter on Human and People's Rights. And finally, the Assembly of Heads of State and Government of the OAU adopted the Charter in 1981 in Banjul (the Gambia) and officially named it the "Banjul Charter".

So far an attempt has been made to define regionalism, to compare regionalism and universalism system, to disclose the European and African human right system. Regionalism phenomena are as old as human history.

It is the organization of states to solve their socio-economical problem in a limited area. As far as human rights are concerned, at present time there are many regional organizations for the purpose of promotion and protection of human rights. In general regional human right system is important for the promotion and protection of human rights at the global level. Thus, it demands recognition from the universal system, like UN.

The concept of human rights should be defined in such a manner as to promote cultural diversities and respect. What are human rights for Europe and USA might not be so in Arab world and Asian context. A good example is the right of homosexuality and gay marriage. Thus, regionalism arrangement on human rights facilitates to formulate a compromise solution to such type of problem.

### Postmodernism

Standards and values are relative to the culture from which they derive so that any attempt to formulate postulates that have grown out of the beliefs or moral codes of one culture must to that extent detract from the applicability of any Declaration of Human Rights to mankind as a whole. As globalization now more rapidly erodes the once stronger traditional notions of sovereignty, domestic jurisdiction, and cultural autonomy, the current debate reflects pains, pride, and memories of humiliating events that are acutely experienced by nations undergoing radical transformation. Recognizing the great diversity of values and their roots in cultures was once one step in the direction of moral condemnation of colonialism and brutal missionary expeditions.

This aim is to analyze the nature of postmodern discourse on human rights. The principal argument is that postmodernism appears to be incompatible with the idea of rights because of its hostility to the conceptions of autonomous subject and universality. On the other hand, the postmodern discourse does not underestimate the "modern" ethical issues like human rights. This brings about two controversial conclusions: the adoption of an unreflective pragmatism by postmodernists towards human rights, and the abandonment of foundationalist approach to rights adopted by some rights theorists. Almost any study concerning postmodernism starts off with an opening remark that postmodernism is an ambiguous and elusive conception.

The rapid urbanization process has created a host of problems. One is the weakening of social order. Older tribal, village, and extended-fairly loyalties are being destroyed, with few off-setting values and other social support systems to take their place. The struggling LDSs are often unable to meet the employment, satisfying, housing, and other needs of the flood of people moving to or being born in the cities. The postmodern society is becoming more and more value free. The postmodern society is marked by discontinuity, catastrophes and paradoxes.

Cultural conflicts are increasing and are understandably more dangerous today than at any other time in history. Postmodernism can make a substantial contribution to interpreting and understanding the importance of Eurocentric economic ideologies and related patterns of self-formation. Postmodernism and social constructionism (or central concepts of these intellectual movements) also have much to offer on issues concerning sustainable development and human rights. Cultural difference needs to be understood, however, if tolerance is to be real it must have limits. No government or people, for example, should do or be allowed to do what European Americans have done to the people and cultures of the American Indians. Conquest is not a right, and no rights follow from conquest.

## Conclusions

The violation of human rights have not been sufficiently reduced, either in number or in seriousness, the attitude of hopeless resignation, the blanket of silence and the absence of remedies are all gradually disappearing; this is an encouraging development, which must be preserved at all costs. Undoubtedly, the more fundamental rights are extended, the more it becomes difficult to satisfy each one of them. Their realization depends on the political system in force; liberal systems are able to give priority to the safeguarding of individual freedoms, and socialist societies give preference to the fulfilment of economic and social rights or some of them.

Following strategies can be followed with a view to improve international human rights:

1. ratification of international human rights instruments;
2. enhancement of enforcement mechanisms;
3. measures for effective national implementation;
4. respect for human rights by parties to the conflict;
5. dissemination of conventions;
6. enactment of penal legislations;
7. translation of treaties into national languages.

Human rights are to be recognized and assisted, not through an external authority, but by the spirit within humanity itself. The great deal remains to be done and, even when national implementation is achieved in formal terms, its success will depend largely on the actual application of the measures taken. The ultimate responsibly to ensure full respect for international human rights rests with governments and individuals. Hence, ratification, interpretation and implementation of treaty, including reservations and statements of interpretation made upon ratification were included in the study. The study also reveals areas where the law is not clear and points to issues which require further clarification, such as the clarification of various rights and ratification of international human rights law. In the light of the achievement to date and the work that remain to be seen as the end but rather as the beginning of a new process aimed at improving understanding of and agreement on the principle and rule of international human rights law.

## NOTES

1. Lori Fsler Damrosch et al., *International Law-Cases and Materials*, 2001 (4th Ed, West Group, A Thompson Company, S.T. Paul Minn), pp. 586-87.
2. Charlotte Ku and Harold K. Jocobson, 'Broaching the Issues', 2002, Ed, Charlotte, *Democratic Accountability and the Use of Force in International law* (New York, Cambridge University Press), pp. 3, 25-26.
3. Geneva conventions and its Additional Protocols to the said conventions.
4. Aricles 3 and 192.
5. *Ibid.*

6. Surath Singh, *Law Relating to Terrorism*, United Law Publishing Pvt.
7. Tokyo Convention, the Hague Convention, and the Montreal Convention.
8. William Schbas, *Introduction to International Criminal Law* (2001, Cambridge University Press), p. 3.
9. Pery Gldraudesm, *Humanitarian Laws* (Ed), 1973, Cherfbassion, USA.
10. Edward M. Wise, *International Criminal Law*, Cases and Materials, Lexs Publishing, p. 18.
11. Illas Bantekas, *International Criminal Law*, 2003, Cavendish Publishing Ltd., p. 5.
12. Gerald Werle, *Principles of Criminal Law*, 2005 (TMC, Asser Press, UK), p. 15.
13. Allison Marston Danner, 2001, 'Constructing A Hierarchy of Crimes in International Criminal Law Strengthening', *Virginia Law Journal*, Vol. 87, No. 3, p. 423.
14. Henry J. Steiner, *International Human Rights in Context*, Oxford University Press, 2000, first ed, p. 783.
15. L.F. Damarosch et. al., *International Law Cases and Materials*, West Group Michigan, 2001, p. 632.

18

# Adam, Eve and "Others" — Analyzing the Right to Survive with Dignity of the Third Sex in India

*Lopamudra Sengupta*

## Introduction

Gender is one of the sensitive barometer through which the plight of human rights in a society can be easily understood. The notion of gender identity becomes significant when one is perceived through his or her gender identity which is often hierarchized in terms of the dominant culture. In India the patriarchal culture has defined and hierarchized gender identities, placing male at the core, and women at the periphery based on sex differences, and idealization of man's natural superiority over the women.

The Hijras in India who are also synonymously termed as kliba, napumsika, "third gender", as provided by a lexicologist of the Vedic era, trytya prakriti (original nature), Sanda (desiccated testicles), kliba, and panda (testicles removed) remained outside the matrix of society's conventional parameter of gender identity. Till the better part of the twentieth century gender studies in India necessarily implied women's studies and her role as a subordinate in a patriarchic world of power relations. At other times, it was studied as a shift from the study of women in isolation from men to the study of women within the context of the social construction of gender.

The other gender, the Hijras who are neither male nor female have all along been ignored left aside or simply not discussed. The major hurdle therefore as witnessed in the 21st century is towards building a healthy and open minded human society in accepting different identities, more specifically divergent sexual and gender identities which often leads to legal, social and cultural discriminations. The inferiorisation of the different groups by dominant groups is not merely an assault on human dignity but results to an implicit marginalization—indeed, often exclusion of these groups from the purview of human rights.

Though it is often assumed that the State in almost all issues act as the major violator of human rights, scant attention is given on society's role in subjugating individual's identity as a human being. The community through its various norms, customs and practices play an important role in acting as a parallel discourse of power. The community thus by creating notions of "identity" violates human rights along lines of gender, religion, caste, etc.

In the following few paragraphs author would try to analyse how social constructions along lines of gender identity act as menace in robbing men from human essentialism.

### Locating the Meaning of Hijra in Tradition

The Third Sex or Eunuchs who are colloquially known as "Hijra" has a fairly long history in the soil of this country. Mention of Hijras dates back to the tales of *Ramayana* and *Mahabharata*. In *Mahabharata* characters like that of Shikhandi portrays image of a man but not fully a man.[1]

A legend in the *Mahabharata* reveals that the son of Arjuna and Nagakanya, is Aravan who was offered to Goddess Kali to ensure the victory in the Kurukshetra war. The only condition that he made was to spend the last night of his life in matrimony. Since no woman was willing to marry one who was doomed to be killed, Krishna assumes the form of a beautiful woman called Mohini and marries him. The hijras of Tamil Nadu consider Aravan their progenitor and call themselves Aravanis.

The term Hijras is said to have Urdu origin—the language the soldiers used in the Mughal Bazzar a combination of Hindi, Persian and Arabic.[2] A Nepali lexicon noted that the word Hijra is derived from the Persian world Hiz. Hiz meant one who is "effeminate", "disdains women", a catamite—colloquially, today known as "lewd", "lascivious".[3] However, though the term 'Hijra' and 'Eunuch' are often used synonymously, dictionary refers to an eunuch as a castrated male.

The existence of hijras and transgender communities can be found throughout the globe. They are variously known as Baklas in the Philippines, Berdaches among American Indian tribes, Serrers in Africa, hijras, Jogappas, Shiv-shaktis and Aravanis in South Asia. They are called as Daejak in Indonesia, where the women's genitals are on the inside and male's on the outside. In some culture the conceptualization of male and female is much more fluid or intermixed effects. Flesh is female and bone male in Nepalese understandings, meaning male and female are mixed in every body. Among the Hua of the Eastern Highlands of Papua New Guinea, male and female substances are transferred between bodies through eating, heterosexual sex and everybody casual contact so that a genetically male person can be classified as female and *vice versa*.[4]

## Social Exclusion and Community Formation

Though presence of hijras is nothing unusual yet their presence in the form of a community in South Asia and especially in India deserves special attention. These people whose sexual organs are not identified as male or female are subjected to all kinds of social oppression and torture. This is done through the *Social Gaze* which despises and ridicules them and treats them as derelicts.

Problems related to the natural born eunuchs are physiological and are related to chromosome. Instead of normal XX (in case of female) and XY (in case of the male) the eunuchs possess chromosomes in excess.[5] They are thought as 'curse' sent from heaven. The families of these individuals suffer from enormous guilt in keeping dirt at home. The look, the attitude, behaviour, makes them feel lonely in a close knit society and gradually feel they are isolated from the mainstream. Their peculiar look, a masculine face on a feminine body, or feminine face on a masculine body attracts 'queer' glances. The curiosity to peep into an unknown body pushes them into the trade of prostitution. Thus, humiliation faced from the society, peer group and family forces them to join the community where their deviant sexuality is accepted and encouraged. They can live a life of their own will and can exercise 'choice' and 'autonomy' over their lives. But true hermaphrodites are statistically quite rare.

According to the report of the All India Hijra Kalyan Sabha, the number of natural born eunuchs in whole India is only 213. The report also states that only one naturally born eunuch is born in every lakh.[6] The community is also composed of individuals who have castrated themselves for earning a living or for various physiological problems. In a book, *Neither Man nor Woman*, Serena Nanda, an American anthropologist mentioned that the hijras she had interviewed informed her that they had joined the community voluntarily.[7]

The history of castration is not new in India. In the book *Invisibles*, Zia Jaffrey draws account from various sources to show how children who often found themselves physically defective felt depressed and frustrated and got themselves castrated on the advice of some eunuchs. The method of castration also reveals crude and inhuman practices. It is usually done by the midwife or "dai ma" who has "no special training". The operation called "nirvana" connoting transcendence is usually done in secret as it is illegal according to the Indian Penal Code.[8] These people are first intoxicated and tied up to a wall with hands tied up at the back. Then with a sharp weapon the testis is cut off. Many die out of this inhuman practice. Those who remain are incorporated within the group and eventually become part of the community.[9]

Apart from the natural born hermaphrodite and castrated males, the community of Hijras in India also comprises of group of people known as transgender, transsexuals and transvestites. The problem with these people are more psychological than physiological. For example, in some cases individuals born with a physical characteristic of one sex has psychological identification with the other. They are known as transsexuals. In some cases individuals derive pleasure from merely wearing the clothes of opposite sex. Unlike transsexuals, the transvestites do not possess a strong desire to alter their physical appearance so that it conforms to that of the desired sex.[10]

During her fieldwork, author met Jayanta Nath a transsexual in his early twenties. Jayanta said people treat him as a circus clown. He questioned whether the mainstream will accept them as they are. Jayanta whose sexual identification is with the opposite sex wants to remain the way he is and would never go for an operation. Like Jayanta there are many who feel that they are trapped in a wrong body. Though some long to change sex through sex reassignment surgery, it is expensive and beyond the reach of average people. He even pointed out that sometimes basic medical care is not available and hospitals turn them back.[11] They remain isolated even in a well-knit society and sometimes develop a language of their own for communication. Facing total "social ostracism" these people join the community to lead a life of their own. They thus enjoy their 'individual right' vis-a-vis their group identity.

These people are thrown into a world where they live from the fear of harsh policing of the borders of 'normal sexuality' as distinct from the 'abnormal' ones. This fear becomes a part of the daily life of these people. There is the fear of being caught by the police, the fear of one's family or colleagues at work discovering your sexuality and the fear that sooner or later the secret will be discovered which could mean a great deal of shame for the person and a possible ruinous impact on his/her future life. The emotion of fear goes hand in hand with the feeling of shame at possessing what society insists are abnormal sexual desires.[12]

## Relevance of Equal Rights in Theory and Practice

Human rights talk of persons born with an equal right to life. However, our attainment of basic property, access to education, financial security brings a change in the life and status of an individual. The person then not merely lives; he lives a decent and dignified life. Human rights ought to ensure all citizens the minimum necessities for a decent life. A "decent" life implies not only a reasonably secure economic situation, but the chance to make autonomous personal choices and participate in public decision-making. This will help create a community in which citizens exhibit concern and respect for one another. As Rhoda Howard observes human rights do not necessitate any particular style of life, but the lack of human rights, whether of personal freedom or basic economic decency and social respect, forecloses choices and leaves individuals vulnerable to a social, atomistic despair.[13]

The third sex who are a disadvantaged group in the society are debarred from all avenues of life, access to education, a decent family life, the right to form a family, their individual opinion, choices and are completely marginalized. It is this act that robs them of their 'creative potentialities'. As B. Belden observes, human rights advocate for the potential development of all human beings—because we all have 'creative potentialities'. Many of us could be wonderful painters, playwrights, novelists, sculptors, composers, dancers, film directors and so on if only our potentialities were recognized, and were given encouragement, training, and support.

By severing ties from their families and social support, society has robbed them of their 'affective potential' to achieve an emotional or spiritual balance in their lives, to become people of good character, to exhibit positive attitudes towards other so as to give them support, assistance pleasure, friendship and love.[14]

The eunuchs are not people who are mentally and emotionally impaired. For a child with Down's syndrome may not have the required skill to learn. But these people may have excellent skill and potentialities in developing oneself to a great painter, dancer, film director, composer, novelist, sculptor and so on. It is also important not to lose sight of the fact that human potentialities are developed with in a web of cultural, economic, and social relationship that are both facilitating and constraining. In case of eunuchs it has been only constraining rather than facilitating. These people are deprived of there families, schools where teachers and non-familial peers could have played crucial roles in the development of one's personality.[15] They enter in work relationships which are often exploitative. Thus, eunuchs who have potentialities for development are deprived of the web of social relationships for their development.

It is precisely this exclusion and the developmental possibilities and aspirations of the excluded that continues to provide the dynamic for the development of human rights when structures, institutions and practices are outpaced by developmental possibilities and aspirations, there arises domination. Domination is the exercise of power that frustrates the development of individuals, segments of society.[16]

## Reinventing a New Space: Search for an Identity

Human rights have always given primacy to the concept of man's dignity. As Alan Gewirth argues that human rights are derivative from human dignity. It is because humans have dignity that they have rights.[17] A sweeping appeal is also noticed in the Preamble of The Universal Human Rights Declaration, which says that the "inherent dignity" is the starting point of the Declaration. Article 2 of the United Nations states that every one is entitled to all the rights set forth in the Declaration without distinction of any kind such as race, colour, sex, language, religion, political or other opinion, national of social origin, property, birth or status. Keeping in toe with the International Law the Constitution of India too adopted in Article 14, laws related to mans equality irrespective of his or her sexual identity.

But for a very long time, the existence of eunuchs as a group was not recognized by the law. They did not have the fundamental right to vote, be counted in the census or have the right to property. After a long struggle the eunuchs were granted voting rights by the Supreme Court in 1986. Eunuchs now enjoy all Constitutional rights and are governed by laws that apply to all.[18] But laws can only melt the tip of the iceberg. The deep rooted social practice for age long years have penetrated deeply in the minds of the people and law can act as an emancipatory tool only if the framework of homophobia cease to exist. As Arvind Narrain observed that it is because of their stigmatized nature of their sexuality that they never found a voice in Nationalist or subaltern histories. The eunuchs were regarded as "scum, the flotsam, jetsam" of India no more than the beasts of the field.[19] The issue of the existence of these people has been silent in ancient India. Most historians of ancient India ranging from Romila Thapar to D.D. Kosambi, exemplify the tradition of silence.[20] In terms of law it is still a grey area. Minor changes for example the acceptance of their identity in passport, has been accepted. Whether the state can provide a legally sanctified space that can 'accommodate' these different gender identities also need to be examined. The eunuchs in India influenced largely by the New Gender Politics, the values of liberty, equality and "individuality". The third sex in India has strongly refuted the various "nomenclatures" associated with their names, like Napumsaka, Kliba, Third Sex, etc. In an age of globalization, the eunuchs have made their voice heard and has broken what Michel Foucault observes, the tradition of silence.[21]

They are now increasingly conscious of their health which is being exploited in sex trade. There is discrimination even in the health care sector and also doctors are ill-equipped to provide information about sexually transmitted diseases or to conduct an examination because of fear, prejudice and ignorance. Their only plea is that they are human beings and not objects of amusement. Thus, through forming groups, NGOs they have occupied a space to fight for the right to non-discrimination.

They are no longer 'Invisibles' but are eager to talk about their problems, face the media, join politics only to be recognized and join the mainstream by refuting their status as 'marginal' They want to be recognized as Noyona, Shanta, Tista....

## NOTES

1. Zia Jaffery, 1996. The Invisibles, a tale of the Eunuchs of India, Vintage Departure, Vintage Books, INC, New York, p. 148.
2. *Ibid.*, p. 31.
3. *Ibid.*, p. 148.
4. China Report, A Journal of East Asian Studies, April to June 2002, p. 187.
5. Ajoy Majumder and Basu Niloy, Bharater Hijra Samaj, Deep Prakasan, Kolkata, January 1997, pp. 23-24.
6. *Ibid.*, p. 16.

7. Serena Nanda, *Neither Man nor Woman: The Hijras of India*, Belmont, Calif, Wardsworth Publishing Company, 1990.
8. Jaffrey Zia, *Op cit.*, p. 58.
9. Majumder Ajoy and Basu Niloy, *Op cit.*, p. 44.
10. *The Asian Age*, "Why is this Man Not a Woman?" 19.12.1999.
11. "Trapped in Wrong Body They too Want Recognition," *The Asian Age*, 14.09.2000.
12. Arvind Narrain, *Queer: Despised Sexuality, Law and Social Change*, pp. 8-9.
13. Howard Rhoda, *Human Rights and the Search for Community*, p. 181.
14. Fields Belden A., *Human Rights for the New Millennium*, Palgrave Macmillan, New York, 2003, p. 74.
15. *Ibid.*, p. 77.
16. *Ibid.*, p. 81.
17. Sarat Austin and Kearns Thomas R., Ed *Human Rights: Concepts Contests*, Contingencies, The University of Michigan Press, 2002, p. 8.
18. A Close Encounter with the Third Kind, Kaberi Dutta, *The Telegraph*, 31.07.1994.
19. Arvind Narrain, *Queer: Despised Sexuality Law and Social Change*, pp. 59-60.
20. Arvind Narrain, *Op cit.*, p. 33.
21. Michel Foucaul, *The History of Sexuality*, Volume (N), Penguin, New York, 1976, p. 27.

# Contributors

**Subrata Sankar Bagchi**, Reader, Department of Anthropology, Bangabasi Evening College, Kolkata.

**Buddhadeb Chaudhuri**, Dr. B.R. Ambedkar Chair Professor in Anthropology, University of Calcutta and Co-ordinator, Human Rights Programme, University of Calcutta.

**Suranjan Das**, Pro-Vice-Chancellor for Academic Affairs, University of Calcutta and Member, University Grants Commission, India.

**Ishita Mukhopadhyay**, Professor, Department of Economics, University of Calcutta and Director, Women Studies Research Centre, University of Calcutta.

**Debi Chatterjee**, Professor, Department of International Relations, Jadavpur University.

**Siddhartha Guha Roy**, Reader, Department of History, Vivekananda College, Kolkata.

**A.K. Ghosh**, Former Director, Zoological Survey of India and Director, Centre for Environment and Development, Kolkata.

**Sumita Sen**, Professor, Department of International Relations, Jadavpur University.

**Tathagata Chakraborty**, Assostant Professor (Selection Grade), Department of Political Science, Bidhannagar College.

**Syamal Chakraborti**, Professor, Department of Chemistry, University of Calcutta.

**Suman Nath**, Research Associate, Indian Instititute of Management, Kolkata.

**Priyadarsini Sengupta**, Senior Lecturer, Department of Anthropology, Bangabasi College.

**Gopalkrishna Chakraborti**, Reader, Department of Anthropology, University of Calcutta.

**Subir Biswas**, Lecturer, Department of Anthropology, University of North Bengal.

**Ganesh Chandra Mallick**, Research Scholar, Department of Anthropology, University of North Bengal.

**Arpita Ghosh**, Lecturer, Human Rights Department, Ramkrishna Sarada Mission College, Kolkata.

**Ahana Datta Mukherjee**, Lecturer, Department of Human Rights, Loreto College, Kolkata.

**Ankita Ghosh**, Lecturer, George College of Management and Science, Kolkata.

**S.K. Nandy**, Senior Researcher, Anthropological Survey of India, Salt Lake City, Kolkata.

**D.K. Adak**, Senior Researcher, Anthropological Survey of India, 27, Jawaharlal Nehru Road, Kolkata.

**Prasenjit Sarkar**, Senior Lecturer, Department of Anthropology, Bangabasi Morning College, Kolkata.

**T.R. Maruthi**, Lecturer in Law, Department of Studies in Law, University of Mysore, Mysore.

**Lopamudra Sengupta**, Reader, Department of Political Science, Bangabasi College, Kolkata.